ON THE INCARNATION

AND

AGAINST THE HEATHEN

by

ST. ATHANASIUS

Contents

ON THE INCARNATION

Chapter 1

Creation and the Fall

(1) In our former book [1] we dealt fully enough with a few of the chief points about the heathen worship of idols, and how those false fears originally arose. We also, by God's grace, briefly indicated that the Word of the Father is Himself divine, that all things that are owe their being to His will and power, and that it is through Him that the Father gives order to creation, by Him that all things are moved, and through Him that they receive their being. Now, Macarius, true lover of Christ, we must take a step further in the faith of our holy religion, and consider also the Word's becoming Man and His divine Appearing in our midst. That mystery the Jews traduce, the Greeks deride, but we adore; and your own love and devotion to the Word also will be the greater, because in His Manhood He seems so little worth. For it is a fact that the more unbelievers pour scorn on Him, so much the more does He make His Godhead evident. The things which they, as men, rule out as impossible, He plainly shows to be possible; that which they deride as unfitting, His goodness makes most fit; and things which these wise-acres laugh at as "human" He by His inherent might declares divine. Thus by what seems His utter poverty and weakness on the cross He overturns the pomp and parade of idols, and quietly and hiddenly wins over the mockers and unbelievers to recognize Him as God.

Now in dealing with these matters it is necessary first to recall what has already been said. You must understand why it is that the Word of the Father, so great and so high, has been made manifest in bodily form. He has not assumed a body as proper to His own nature, far from it, for as the Word He is without body. He has been manifested in a human body for this reason only, out of the love and goodness of His Father, for the salvation of us men. We will begin, then, with the creation of the world and with God its Maker, for the first fact that you must grasp is this: the renewal of creation has been wrought by the Self-same Word Who made it in the beginning. There is thus no inconsistency between creation and salvation for the One Father has employed the same Agent for both works, effecting the salvation of the world through the same Word Who made it in the beginning.

(2) In regard to the making of the universe and the creation of all things there have been various opinions, and each person has propounded the theory that suited his own taste. For instance, some say that all things are self-originated and, so to speak, haphazard. The Epicureans are among these; they deny that there is any Mind behind the universe at all. This view is contrary to all the facts of experience, their own existence included. For if all things had come into being in this automatic fashion, instead of being the outcome of Mind, though they existed, they would all be uniform and without distinction. In the universe everything would be sun or moon or whatever it was, and in the human body the whole would be hand or eye or foot. But in point of fact the sun and the moon and the earth are all different things, and even within the human body there are different members, such as foot and hand and head. This distinctness of things argues not a spontaneous generation but a prevenient Cause; and from that Cause we can apprehend God, the Designer and Maker of all.

Others take the view expressed by Plato, that giant among the Greeks. He said that God had made all things out of pre-existent and uncreated matter, just as the carpenter makes things only out of wood that already exists. But those who hold this view do not realize that to deny that God is Himself the Cause of matter is to impute limitation to Him, just as it is undoubtedly a limitation on the part of the carpenter that he can make nothing unless he has the wood. How could God be called Maker and Artificer if His ability to make depended on some other cause, namely on matter itself? If He only worked up existing matter and did not Himself bring matter into being, He would be not the Creator but only a craftsman.

Then, again, there is the theory of the Gnostics, who have invented for themselves an Artificer of all things other than the Father of our Lord Jesus Christ. These simply shut their eyes to the obvious meaning of Scripture. For instance, the Lord, having reminded the Jews of the statement in Genesis, "He Who created them in the beginning made them male and female . . . ," and having shown that for that reason a man should leave his parents and cleave to his wife, goes on to say with reference to the Creator, "What therefore God has joined together, let no man put asunder." [2] How can they get a creation independent of the Father out of that? And, again, St. John, speaking all inclusively, says, "All things became by Him and without Him came nothing into being." [3] How then could the Artificer be someone different, other than the Father of Christ?

(3) Such are the notions which men put forward. But the impiety of their foolish talk is plainly declared by the divine teaching of the Christian faith. From it we know that, because there is Mind behind the universe, it did not originate itself; because God is infinite, not finite, it was not made from pre-existent matter, but out of nothing and out of non-existence absolute and utter God brought it into being through the Word. He says as much in Genesis: "In the beginning God created the heavens and the earth; [4] and again through that most helpful book The Shepherd, "Believe thou first and foremost that there is One God Who created and arranged all things and brought them out of non-existence into being." [5] Paul also indicates the same thing when he says, "By faith we understand that the worlds were framed by the Word of God, so that the things which we see now did not come into being out of things which had previously appeared." [6] For God is good--or rather, of all goodness He is Fountainhead, and it is impossible for one who is good to be mean or grudging about anything. Grudging existence to none therefore, He made all things out of nothing through His own Word, our Lord Jesus Christ and of all these His earthly creatures He reserved especial mercy for the race of men. Upon them, therefore, upon men who, as animals, were essentially impermanent, He bestowed a grace which other creatures lacked-- namely the impress of His own Image, a share in the reasonable being of the very Word Himself, so that, reflecting Him and themselves becoming reasonable and expressing the Mind of God even as He does, though in limited degree they might continue for ever in the blessed and only true life of the saints in paradise. But since the will of man could turn either way, God secured this grace that He had given by making it conditional from the first upon two things--namely, a law and a place. He set them in His own paradise, and laid upon them a

single prohibition. If they guarded the grace and retained the loveliness of their original innocence, then the life of paradise should be theirs, without sorrow, pain or care, and after it the assurance of immortality in heaven. But if they went astray and became vile, throwing away their birthright of beauty, then they would come under the natural law of death and live no longer in paradise, but, dying outside of it, continue in death and in corruption. This is what Holy Scripture tells us, proclaiming the command of God, "Of every tree that is in the garden thou shalt surely eat, but of the tree of the knowledge of good and evil ye shall not eat, but in the day that ye do eat, ye shall surely die." [7] "Ye shall surely die"--not just die only, but remain in the state of death and of corruption.

(4) You may be wondering why we are discussing the origin of men when we set out to talk about the Word's becoming Man. The former subject is relevant to the latter for this reason: it was our sorry case that caused the Word to come down, our transgression that called out His love for us, so that He made haste to help us and to appear among us. It is we who were the cause of His taking human form, and for our salvation that in His great love He was both born and manifested in a human body. For God had made man thus (that is, as an embodied spirit), and had willed that he should remain in incorruption. But men, having turned from the contemplation of God to evil of their own devising, had come inevitably under the law of death. Instead of remaining in the state in which God had created them, they were in process of becoming corrupted entirely, and death had them completely under its dominion. For the transgression of the commandment was making them turn back again according to their nature; and as they had at the beginning come into being out of non-existence, so were they now on the way to returning, through corruption, to non-existence again. The presence and love of the Word had called them into being; inevitably, therefore when they lost the knowledge of God, they lost existence with it; for it is God alone Who exists, evil is non-being, the negation and antithesis of good. By nature, of course, man is mortal, since he was made from nothing; but he bears also the Likeness of Him Who is, and if he preserves that Likeness through constant contemplation, then his nature is deprived of its power and he remains incorrupt. So is it affirmed in Wisdom: "The keeping of His laws is the assurance of incorruption." [8] And being incorrupt, he would be henceforth as God, as Holy Scripture says, "I have said, Ye are gods

and sons of the Highest all of you: but ye die as men and fall as one of the princes." [9]

(5) This, then, was the plight of men. God had not only made them out of nothing, but had also graciously bestowed on them His own life by the grace of the Word. Then, turning from eternal things to things corruptible, by counsel of the devil, they had become the cause of their own corruption in death; for, as I said before, though they were by nature subject to corruption, the grace of their union with the Word made them capable of escaping from the natural law, provided that they retained the beauty of innocence with which they were created. That is to say, the presence of the Word with them shielded them even from natural corruption, as also Wisdom says: "God created man for incorruption and as an image of His own eternity; but by envy of the devil death entered into the world." [10] When this happened, men began to die, and corruption ran riot among them and held sway over them to an even more than natural degree, because it was the penalty of which God had forewarned them for transgressing the commandment. Indeed, they had in their sinning surpassed all limits; for, having invented wickedness in the beginning and so involved themselves in death and corruption, they had gone on gradually from bad to worse, not stopping at any one kind of evil, but continually, as with insatiable appetite, devising new kinds of sins. Adulteries and thefts were everywhere, murder and rapine filled the earth, law was disregarded in corruption and injustice, all kinds of iniquities were perpetrated by all, both singly and in common. Cities were warring with cities, nations were rising against nations, and the whole earth was rent with factions and battles, while each strove to outdo the other in wickedness. Even crimes contrary to nature were not unknown, but as the martyr-apostle of Christ says: "Their women changed the natural use into that which is against nature; and the men also, leaving the natural use of the woman, flamed out in lust towards each other, perpetrating shameless acts with their own sex, and receiving in their own persons the due recompense of their pervertedness." [11]

[1] i.e. the Contra Gentes.
[2] Matt. xix. 4-6
[3] John i. 3
[4] Gen. i. 1
[5] The Shepherd of Hermas, Book II. I
[6] Heb. xi. 3
[7] Gen. ii. 16 f.

[8] Wisdom vi. 18
[9] Psalm lxxxii. 6 f.
[10] Wisdom ii. 23 f.
[11] Rom. i. 26 f.

Chapter 2

The Divine Dilemma and its Solution in the Incarnation

(6) We saw in the last chapter that, because death and corruption were gaining ever firmer hold on them, the human race was in process of destruction. Man, who was created in God's image and in his possession of reason reflected the very Word Himself, was disappearing, and the work of God was being undone. The law of death, which followed from the Transgression, prevailed upon us, and from it there was no escape. The thing that was happening was in truth both monstrous and unfitting. It would, of course, have been unthinkable that God should go back upon His word and that man, having transgressed, should not die; but it was equally monstrous that beings which once had shared the nature of the Word should perish and turn back again into non-existence through corruption. It was unworthy of the goodness of God that creatures made by Him should be brought to nothing through the deceit wrought upon man by the devil; and it was supremely unfitting that the work of God in mankind should disappear, either through their own negligence or through the deceit of evil spirits. As, then, the creatures whom He had created reasonable, like the Word, were in fact perishing, and such noble works were on the road to ruin, what then was God, being Good, to do? Was He to let corruption and death have their way with them? In that case, what was the use of having made them in the beginning? Surely it would have been better never to have been created at all than, having been created, to be neglected and perish; and, besides that, such indifference to the ruin of His own work before His very eyes would argue not goodness in God but limitation, and that far more than if He had never created men at all. It was impossible, therefore, that God should leave man to be carried off by corruption, because it would be unfitting and unworthy of Himself.

(7) Yet, true though this is, it is not the whole matter. As we have already noted, it was unthinkable that God, the Father of Truth, should go back upon His word regarding death in order to ensure our continued existence. He could not falsify Himself; what, then, was God to do? Was He to demand repentance from men for their transgression? You might say that that was worthy of God, and argue further that, as through the Transgression they became subject to corruption, so through repentance they might return to incorruption again. But repentance would not guard the Divine consistency, for, if death did not hold dominion over men, God would still remain untrue. Nor does repentance recall men from what is according to their nature; all that it does is to make them cease from sinning. Had it been a case of a trespass only, and not of a subsequent corruption, repentance would have been well enough; but when once transgression had begun men came under the power of the corruption proper to their nature and were bereft of the grace which belonged to them as creatures in the Image of God. No, repentance could not meet the case. What--or rather Who was it that was needed for such grace and such recall as we required? Who, save the Word of God Himself, Who also in the beginning had made all things out of nothing? His part it was, and His alone, both to bring again the corruptible to incorruption and to maintain for the Father His consistency of character with all. For He alone, being Word of the Father and above all, was in consequence both able to recreate all, and worthy to suffer on behalf of all and to be an ambassador for all with the Father.

(8) For this purpose, then, the incorporeal and incorruptible and immaterial Word of God entered our world. In one sense, indeed, He was not far from it before, for no part of creation had ever been without Him Who, while ever abiding in union with the Father, yet fills all things that are. But now He entered the world in a new way, stooping to our level in His love and Self-revealing to us. He saw the reasonable race, the race of men that, like Himself, expressed the Father's Mind, wasting out of existence, and death reigning over all in corruption. He saw that corruption held us all the closer, because it was the penalty for the Transgression; He saw, too, how unthinkable it would be for the law to be repealed before it was fulfilled. He saw how unseemly it was that the very things of which He Himself was the Artificer should be disappearing. He saw how the surpassing wickedness of men was mounting up against them; He saw also their universal liability to

death. All this He saw and, pitying our race, moved with compassion for our limitation, unable to endure that death should have the mastery, rather than that His creatures should perish and the work of His Father for us men come to nought, He took to Himself a body, a human body even as our own. Nor did He will merely to become embodied or merely to appear; had that been so, He could have revealed His divine majesty in some other and better way. No, He took our body, and not only so, but He took it directly from a spotless, stainless virgin, without the agency of human father--a pure body, untainted by intercourse with man. He, the Mighty One, the Artificer of all, Himself prepared this body in the virgin as a temple for Himself, and took it for His very own, as the instrument through which He was known and in which He dwelt. Thus, taking a body like our own, because all our bodies were liable to the corruption of death, He surrendered His body to death instead of all, and offered it to the Father. This He did out of sheer love for us, so that in His death all might die, and the law of death thereby be abolished because, having fulfilled in His body that for which it was appointed, it was thereafter voided of its power for men. This He did that He might turn again to incorruption men who had turned back to corruption, and make them alive through death by the appropriation of His body and by the grace of His resurrection. Thus He would make death to disappear from them as utterly as straw from fire.

(9) The Word perceived that corruption could not be got rid of otherwise than through death; yet He Himself, as the Word, being immortal and the Father's Son, was such as could not die. For this reason, therefore, He assumed a body capable of death, in order that it, through belonging to the Word Who is above all, might become in dying a sufficient exchange for all, and, itself remaining incorruptible through His indwelling, might thereafter put an end to corruption for all others as well, by the grace of the resurrection. It was by surrendering to death the body which He had taken, as an offering and sacrifice free from every stain, that He forthwith abolished death for His human brethren by the offering of the equivalent. For naturally, since the Word of God was above all, when He offered His own temple and bodily instrument as a substitute for the life of all, He fulfilled in death all that was required. Naturally also, through this union of the immortal Son of God with our human nature, all men were clothed with incorruption in the promise of the resurrection. For the solidarity of mankind is such that, by virtue of the Word's indwelling in a single human body, the corrup-

tion which goes with death has lost its power over all. You know how it is when some great king enters a large city and dwells in one of its houses; because of his dwelling in that single house, the whole city is honored, and enemies and robbers cease to molest it. Even so is it with the King of all; He has come into our country and dwelt in one body amidst the many, and in consequence the designs of the enemy against mankind have been foiled and the corruption of death, which formerly held them in its power, has simply ceased to be. For the human race would have perished utterly had not the Lord and Savior of all, the Son of God, come among us to put an end to death.

(10) This great work was, indeed, supremely worthy of the goodness of God. A king who has founded a city, so far from neglecting it when through the carelessness of the inhabitants it is attacked by robbers, avenges it and saves it from destruction, having regard rather to his own honor than to the people's neglect. Much more, then, the Word of the All-good Father was not unmindful of the human race that He had called to be; but rather, by the offering of His own body He abolished the death which they had incurred, and corrected their neglect by His own teaching. Thus by His own power He restored the whole nature of man. The Savior's own inspired disciples assure us of this. We read in one place: "For the love of Christ constraineth us, because we thus judge that, if One died on behalf of all, then all died, and He died for all that we should no longer live unto ourselves, but unto Him who died and rose again from the dead, even our Lord Jesus Christ." [12] And again another says: "But we behold Him Who hath been made a little lower than the angels, even Jesus, because of the suffering of death crowned with glory and honor, that by the grace of God He should taste of death on behalf of every man." The same writer goes on to point out why it was necessary for God the Word and none other to become Man: "For it became Him, for Whom are all things and through Whom are all things, in bringing many sons unto glory, to make the Author of their salvation perfect through suffering." [13] He means that the rescue of mankind from corruption was the proper part only of Him Who made them in the beginning. He points out also that the Word assumed a human body, expressly in order that He might offer it in sacrifice for other like bodies: "Since then the children are sharers in flesh and blood, He also Himself assumed the same, in order that through death He might bring to nought Him that hath the power of death, that is to say, the Devil, and might rescue those who all their lives were enslaved by the fear of death." [14] For by the sacrifice of

His own body He did two things: He put an end to the law of death which barred our way; and He made a new beginning of life for us, by giving us the hope of resurrection. By man death has gained its power over men; by the Word made Man death has been destroyed and life raised up anew. That is what Paul says, that true servant of Christ: "For since by man came death, by man came also the resurrection of the dead. Just as in Adam all die, even so in Christ shall all be made alive," [15] and so forth. Now, therefore, when we die we no longer do so as men condemned to death, but as those who are even now in process of rising we await the general resurrection of all, "which in its own times He shall show," [16] even God Who wrought it and bestowed it on us.

This, then, is the first cause of the Savior's becoming Man. There are, however, other things which show how wholly fitting is His blessed presence in our midst; and these we must now go on to consider.

[12] 2 Cor. v. 14 f.
[13] Heb. ii. 9 ff.
[14] Heb. ii. 14 f.
[15] 1 Cor. xv. 21 f.
[16] 1 Tim. vi. 15

Chapter 3

The Divine Dilemma and its Solution in the Incarnation
(continued)

(11) When God the Almighty was making mankind through His own
Word, He perceived that they, owing to the limitation of their nature,
could not of themselves have any knowledge of their Artificer, the Incorporeal and Uncreated. He took pity on them, therefore, and did not
leave them destitute of the knowledge of Himself, lest their very existence should prove purposeless. For of what use is existence to the
creature if it cannot know its Maker? How could men be reasonable
beings if they had no knowledge of the Word and Reason of the Father, through Whom they had received their being? They would be no
better than the beasts, had they no knowledge save of earthly things;
and why should God have made them at all, if He had not intended
them to know Him? But, in fact, the good God has given them a share
in His own Image, that is, in our Lord Jesus Christ, and has made even
themselves after the same Image and Likeness. Why? Simply in order
that through this gift of Godlikeness in themselves they may be able to
perceive the Image Absolute, that is the Word Himself, and through
Him to apprehend the Father; which knowledge of their Maker is for
men the only really happy and blessed life.

But, as we have already seen, men, foolish as they are, thought little of
the grace they had received, and turned away from God. They defiled
their own soul so completely that they not only lost their apprehension
of God, but invented for themselves other gods of various kinds. They
fashioned idols for themselves in place of the truth and reverenced
things that are not, rather than God Who is, as St. Paul says, "worshipping the creature rather than the Creator." [17] Moreover, and much
worse, they transferred the honor which is due to God to material ob-

jects such as wood and stone, and also to man; and further even than that they went, as we said in our former book. Indeed, so impious were they that they worshipped evil spirits as gods in satisfaction of their lusts. They sacrificed brute beasts and immolated men, as the just due of these deities, thereby bringing themselves more and more under their insane control. Magic arts also were taught among them, oracles in sundry places led men astray, and the cause of everything in human life was traced to the stars as though nothing existed but that which could be seen. In a word, impiety and lawlessness were everywhere, and neither God nor His Word was known. Yet He had not hidden Himself from the sight of men nor given the knowledge of Himself in one way only; but rather He had unfolded it in many forms and by many ways.

(12) God knew the limitation of mankind, you see; and though the grace of being made in His Image was sufficient to give them knowledge of the Word and through Him of the Father, as a safeguard against their neglect of this grace, He provided the works of creation also as means by which the Maker might be known. Nor was this all. Man's neglect of the indwelling grace tends ever to increase; and against this further frailty also God made provision by giving them a law, and by sending prophets, men whom they knew. Thus, if they were tardy in looking up to heaven, they might still gain knowledge of their Maker from those close at hand; for men can learn directly about higher things from other men. Three ways thus lay open to them, by which they might obtain the knowledge of God. They could look up into the immensity of heaven, and by pondering the harmony of creation come to know its Ruler, the Word of the Father, Whose all-ruling providence makes known the Father to all. Or, if this was beyond them, they could converse with holy men, and through them learn to know God, the Artificer of all things, the Father of Christ, and to recognize the worship of idols as the negation of the truth and full of all impiety. Or else, in the third place, they could cease from lukewarmness and lead a good life merely by knowing the law. For the law was not given only for the Jews, nor was it solely for their sake that God sent the prophets, though it was to the Jews that they were sent and by the Jews that they were persecuted. The law and the prophets were a sacred school of the knowledge of God and the conduct of the spiritual life for the whole world.

So great, indeed, were the goodness and the love of God. Yet men, bowed down by the pleasures of the moment and by the frauds and illusions of the evil spirits, did not lift up their heads towards the truth. So burdened were they with their wickednesses that they seemed rather to be brute beasts than reasonable men, reflecting the very Likeness of the Word.

(13) What was God to do in face of this dehumanising of mankind, this universal hiding of the knowledge of Himself by the wiles of evil spirits? Was He to keep silence before so great a wrong and let men go on being thus deceived and kept in ignorance of Himself? If so, what was the use of having made them in His own Image originally? It would surely have been better for them always to have been brutes, rather than to revert to that condition when once they had shared the nature of the Word. Again, things being as they were, what was the use of their ever having had the knowledge of God? Surely it would have been better for God never to have bestowed it, than that men should subsequently be found unworthy to receive it. Similarly, what possible profit could it be to God Himself, Who made men, if when made they did not worship Him, but regarded others as their makers? This would be tantamount to His having made them for others and not for Himself. Even an earthly king, though he is only a man, does not allow lands that he has colonized to pass into other hands or to desert to other rulers, but sends letters and friends and even visits them himself to recall them to their allegiance, rather than allow His work to be undone. How much more, then, will God be patient and painstaking with His creatures, that they be not led astray from Him to the service of those that are not, and that all the more because such error means for them sheer ruin, and because it is not right that those who had once shared His Image should be destroyed.

What, then, was God to do? What else could He possibly do, being God, but renew His Image in mankind, so that through it men might once more come to know Him? And how could this be done save by the coming of the very Image Himself, our Savior Jesus Christ? Men could not have done it, for they are only made after the Image; nor could angels have done it, for they are not the images of God. The Word of God came in His own Person, because it was He alone, the Image of the Father Who could recreate man made after the Image.

In order to effect this re-creation, however, He had first to do away with death and corruption. Therefore He assumed a human body, in order that in it death might once for all be destroyed, and that men might be renewed according to the Image. The Image of the Father only was sufficient for this need. Here is an illustration to prove it.

(14) You know what happens when a portrait that has been painted on a panel becomes obliterated through external stains. The artist does not throw away the panel, but the subject of the portrait has to come and sit for it again, and then the likeness is re-drawn on the same material. Even so was it with the All-holy Son of God. He, the Image of the Father, came and dwelt in our midst, in order that He might renew mankind made after Himself, and seek out His lost sheep, even as He says in the Gospel: "I came to seek and to save that which was lost. [18] This also explains His saying to the Jews: "Except a man be born anew . . ." [19] a He was not referring to a man's natural birth from his mother, as they thought, but to the re-birth and re-creation of the soul in the Image of God.

Nor was this the only thing which only the Word could do. When the madness of idolatry and irreligion filled the world and the knowledge of God was hidden, whose part was it to teach the world about the Father? Man's, would you say? But men cannot run everywhere over the world, nor would their words carry sufficient weight if they did, nor would they be, unaided, a match for the evil spirits. Moreover, since even the best of men were confused and blinded by evil, how could they convert the souls and minds of others? You cannot put straight in others what is warped in yourself. Perhaps you will say, then, that creation was enough to teach men about the Father. But if that had been so, such great evils would never have occurred. Creation was there all the time, but it did not prevent men from wallowing in error. Once more, then, it was the Word of God, Who sees all that is in man and moves all things in creation, Who alone could meet the needs of the situation. It was His part and His alone, Whose ordering of the universe reveals the Father, to renew the same teaching. But how was He to do it? By the same means as before, perhaps you will say, that is, through the works of creation. But this was proven insufficient. Men had neglected to consider the heavens before, and now they were looking in the opposite direction. Wherefore, in all naturalness and fitness, desiring to do good to men, as Man He dwells, taking to Himself a body like the rest; and through His actions done in that body, as it were on their own level, He teaches those who would not learn by other means to know Himself, the Word of God, and through Him the Father.

(15) He deals with them as a good teacher with his pupils, coming down to their level and using simple means. St. Paul says as much: "Because in the wisdom of God the world in its wisdom knew not God, God thought fit through the simplicity of the News proclaimed to save those who believe." [20] Men had turned from the contemplation of God above, and were looking for Him in the opposite direction, down among created things and things of sense. The Savior of us all, the Word of God, in His great love took to Himself a body and moved as Man among men, meeting their senses, so to speak, half way. He became Himself an object for the senses, so that those who were seeking God in sensible things might apprehend the Father through the works which He, the Word of God, did in the body. Human and human minded as men were, therefore, to whichever side they looked in the sensible world they found themselves taught the truth. Were they awe-stricken by creation? They beheld it confessing Christ as Lord. Did their minds tend to regard men as Gods? The uniqueness of the Savior's works marked Him, alone of men, as Son of God. Were they drawn to evil spirits? They saw them driven out by the Lord and learned that the Word of God alone was God and that the evil spirits were not gods at all. Were they inclined to hero-worship and the cult of the dead? Then the fact that the Savior had risen from the dead showed them how false these other deities were, and that the Word of the Father is the one true Lord, the Lord even of death. For this reason was He both born and manifested as Man, for this He died and rose, in order that, eclipsing by His works all other human deeds, He might recall men from all the paths of error to know the Father. As He says Himself, "I came to seek and to save that which was lost." [21]

(16) When, then, the minds of men had fallen finally to the level of sensible things, the Word submitted to appear in a body, in order that He, as Man, might center their senses on Himself, and convince them through His human acts that He Himself is not man only but also God, the Word and Wisdom of the true God. This is what Paul wants to tell us when he says: "That ye, being rooted and grounded in love, may be strong to apprehend with all the saints what is the length and breadth and height and depth, and to know the love of God that surpasses knowledge, so that ye may be filled unto all the fullness of God." [22] The Self-revealing of the Word is in every dimension--above, in crea-

tion; below, in the Incarnation; in the depth, in Hades; in the breadth, throughout the world. All things have been filled with the knowledge of God.

For this reason He did not offer the sacrifice on behalf of all immediately He came, for if He had surrendered His body to death and then raised it again at once He would have ceased to be an object of our senses. Instead of that, He stayed in His body and let Himself be seen in it, doing acts and giving signs which showed Him to be not only man, but also God the Word. There were thus two things which the Savior did for us by becoming Man. He banished death from us and made us anew; and, invisible and imperceptible as in Himself He is, He became visible through His works and revealed Himself as the Word of the Father, the Ruler and King of the whole creation.

(17) There is a paradox in this last statement which we must now examine. The Word was not hedged in by His body, nor did His presence in the body prevent His being present elsewhere as well. When He moved His body He did not cease also to direct the universe by His Mind and might. No. The marvelous truth is, that being the Word, so far from being Himself contained by anything, He actually contained all things Himself. In creation He is present everywhere, yet is distinct in being from it; ordering, directing, giving life to all, containing all, yet is He Himself the Uncontained, existing solely in His Father. As with the whole, so also is it with the part. Existing in a human body, to which He Himself gives life, He is still Source of life to all the universe, present in every part of it, yet outside the whole; and He is revealed both through the works of His body and through His activity in the world. It is, indeed, the function of soul to behold things that are outside the body, but it cannot energize or move them. A man cannot transport things from one place to another, for instance, merely by thinking about them; nor can you or I move the sun and the stars just by sitting at home and looking at them. With the Word of God in His human nature, however, it was otherwise. His body was for Him not a limitation, but an instrument, so that He was both in it and in all things, and outside all things, resting in the Father alone. At one and the same time--this is the wonder--as Man He was living a human life, and as Word He was sustaining the life of the universe, and as Son He was in constant union with the Father. Not even His birth from a virgin, therefore, changed Him in any way, nor was He defiled by being in the body. Rather, He sanctified the body by being in it. For His be-

ing in everything does not mean that He shares the nature of everything, only that He gives all things their being and sustains them in it. Just as the sun is not defiled by the contact of its rays with earthly objects, but rather enlightens and purifies them, so He Who made the sun is not defiled by being made known in a body, but rather the body is cleansed and quickened by His indwelling, "Who did no sin, neither was guile found in His mouth." [23]

(18) You must understand, therefore, that when writers on this sacred theme speak of Him as eating and drinking and being born, they mean that the body, as a body, was born and sustained with the food proper to its nature; while God the Word, Who was united with it, was at the same time ordering the universe and revealing Himself through His bodily acts as not man only but God. Those acts are rightly said to be His acts, because the body which did them did indeed belong to Him and none other; moreover, it was right that they should be thus attributed to Him as Man, in order to show that His body was a real one and not merely an appearance. From such ordinary acts as being born and taking food, He was recognized as being actually present in the body; but by the extraordinary acts which He did through the body He proved Himself to be the Son of God. That is the meaning of His words to the unbelieving Jews: "If I do not the works of My Father, believe Me not; but if I do, even if ye believe not Me, believe My works, that ye may know that the Father is in Me and I in the Father." [24]

Invisible in Himself, He is known from the works of creation; so also, when His Godhead is veiled in human nature, His bodily acts still declare Him to be not man only, but the Power and Word of God. To speak authoritatively to evil spirits, for instance, and to drive them out, is not human but divine; and who could see-Him curing all the diseases to which mankind is prone, and still deem Him mere man and not also God? He cleansed lepers, He made the lame to walk, He opened the ears of the deaf and the eyes of the blind, there was no sickness or weakness that-He did not drive away. Even the most casual observer can see that these were acts of God. The healing of the man born blind, for instance, who but the Father and Artificer of man, the Controller of his whole being, could thus have restored the faculty denied at birth? He Who did thus must surely be Himself the Lord of birth. This is proved also at the outset of His becoming Man. He formed His own body from the virgin; and that is no small proof of

His Godhead, since He Who made that was the Maker of all else. And would not anyone infer from the fact of that body being begotten of a virgin only, without human father, that He Who appeared in it was also the Maker and Lord of all beside?

Again, consider the miracle at Cana. Would not anyone who saw the substance of water transmuted into wine understand that He Who did it was the Lord and Maker of the water that He changed? It was for the same reason that He walked on the sea as on dry land--to prove to the onlookers that He had mastery over all. And the feeding of the multitude, when He made little into much, so that from five loaves five thousand mouths were filled--did not that prove Him none other than the very Lord Whose Mind is over all?

[17] Rom. i. 25
[18] Luke xix. 10
[19] John iii. 3
[20] 1 Cor. i. 21
[21] Luke xix. 10
[22] Eph. iii. 17 ff.
[23] 1 Peter ii. 22
[24] John x. 37-38

Chapter 4

The Death of Christ

(19) All these things the Savior thought fit to do, so that, recognizing His bodily acts as works of God, men who were blind to His presence in creation might regain knowledge of the Father. For, as I said before, who that saw His authority over evil spirits and their response to it could doubt that He was, indeed, the Son, the Wisdom and the Power of God? Even the very creation broke silence at His behest and, marvelous to relate, confessed with one voice before the cross, that monument of victory, that He Who suffered thereon in the body was not man only, but Son of God and Savior of all. The sun veiled his face, the earth quaked, the mountains were rent asunder, all men were stricken with awe. These things showed that Christ on the cross was God, and that all creation was His slave and was bearing witness by its fear to the presence of its Master.

Thus, then, God the Word revealed Himself to men through His works. We must next consider the end of His earthly life and the nature of His bodily death. This is, indeed, the very center of our faith, and everywhere you hear men speak of it; by it, too, no less than by His other acts, Christ is revealed as God and Son of God.

(20) We have dealt as far as circumstances and our own understanding permit with the reason for His bodily manifestation. We have seen that to change the corruptible to incorruption was proper to none other than the Savior Himself, Who in the beginning made all things out of nothing; that only the Image of the Father could re-create the likeness of the Image in men, that none save our Lord Jesus Christ could give to mortals immortality, and that only the Word Who orders all things and is alone the Father's true and sole-begotten Son could teach men about

Him and abolish the worship of idols But beyond all this, there was a debt owing which must needs be paid; for, as I said before, all men were due to die. Here, then, is the second reason why the Word dwelt among us, namely that having proved His Godhead by His works, He might offer the sacrifice on behalf of all, surrendering His own temple to death in place of all, to settle man's account with death and free him from the primal transgression. In the same act also He showed Himself mightier than death, displaying His own body incorruptible as the first-fruits of the resurrection.

You must not be surprised if we repeat ourselves in dealing with this subject. We are speaking of the good pleasure of God and of the things which He in His loving wisdom thought fit to do, and it is better to put the same thing in several ways than to run the risk of leaving something out. The body of the Word, then, being a real human body, in spite of its having been uniquely formed from a virgin, was of itself mortal and, like other bodies, liable to death. But the indwelling of the Word loosed it from this natural liability, so that corruption could not touch it. Thus it happened that two opposite marvels took place at once: the death of all was consummated in the Lord's body; yet, because the Word was in it, death and corruption were in the same act utterly abolished. Death there had to be, and death for all, so that the due of all might be paid. Wherefore, the Word, as I said, being Himself incapable of death, assumed a mortal body, that He might offer it as His own in place of all, and suffering for the sake of all through His union with it, " might bring to nought Him that had the power of death, that is, the devil, and might deliver them who all their lifetime were enslaved by the fear of death." [25]

(21) Have no fears then. Now that the common Savior of all has died on our behalf, we who believe in Christ no longer die, as men died aforetime, in fulfillment of the threat of the law. That condemnation has come to an end; and now that, by the grace of the resurrection, corruption has been banished and done away, we are loosed from our mortal bodies in God's good time for each, so that we may obtain thereby a better resurrection. Like seeds cast into the earth, we do not perish in our dissolution, but like them shall rise again, death having been brought to nought by the grace of the Savior. That is why blessed Paul, through whom we all have surety of the resurrection, says: "This corruptible must put on incorruption and this mortal must put on immortality; but when this corruptible shall have put on incorruption and

this mortal shall have put on immortality, then shall be brought to pass the saying that is written, 'Death is swallowed up in victory. O Death, where is thy sting? O Grave, where is thy victory?" [26]

"Well then," some people may say, "if the essential thing was that He should surrender His body to death in place of all, why did He not do so as Man privately, without going to the length of public crucifixion? Surely it would have been more suitable for Him to have laid aside His body with honor than to endure so shameful a death." But look at this argument closely, and see how merely human it is, whereas what the Savior did was truly divine and worthy of His Godhead for several reasons. The first is this. The death of men under ordinary circumstances is the result of their natural weakness. They are essentially impermanent, so after a time they fall ill and when worn out they die. But the Lord is not like that. He is not weak, He is the Power of God and Word of God and Very Life Itself. If He had died quietly in His bed like other men it would have looked as if He did so in accordance with His nature, and as though He was indeed no more than other men. But because He was Himself Word and Life and Power His body was made strong, and because the death had to be accomplished, He took the occasion of perfecting His sacrifice not from Himself, but from others. How could He fall sick, Who had healed others? Or how could that body weaken and fail by means of which others are made strong? Here, again, you may say, "Why did He not prevent death, as He did sickness?" Because it was precisely in order to be able to die that He had taken a body, and to prevent the death would have been to impede the resurrection. And as to the unsuitability of sickness for His body, as arguing weakness, you may say, "Did He then not hunger?" Yes, He hungered, because that was the property of His body, but He did not die of hunger because He Whose body hungered was the Lord. Similarly, though He died to ransom all, He did not see corruption. His body rose in perfect soundness, for it was the body of none other than the Life Himself.

(22) Someone else might say, perhaps, that it would have been better for the Lord to have avoided the designs of the Jews against Him, and so to have guarded His body from death altogether. But see how unfitting this also would have been for Him. Just as it would not have been fitting for Him to give His body to death by His own hand, being Word and being Life, so also it was not consonant with Himself that He should avoid the death inflicted by others. Rather, He pursued it to

the uttermost, and in pursuance of His nature neither laid aside His body of His own accord nor escaped the plotting Jews. And this action showed no limitation or weakness in the Word; for He both waited for death in order to make an end of it, and hastened to accomplish it as an offering on behalf of all. Moreover, as it was the death of all mankind that the Savior came to accomplish, not His own, He did not lay aside His body by an individual act of dying, for to Him, as Life, this simply did not belong; but He accepted death at the hands of men, thereby completely to destroy it in His own body.

There are some further considerations which enable one to understand why the Lord's body had such an end. The supreme object of His coming was to bring about the resurrection of the body. This was to be the monument to His victory over death, the assurance to all that He had Himself conquered corruption and that their own bodies also would eventually be incorrupt; and it was in token of that and as a pledge of the future resurrection that He kept His body incorrupt. But there again, if His body had fallen sick and the Word had left it in that condition, how unfitting it would have been! Should He Who healed the bodies of others neglect to keep His own in health? How would His miracles of healing be believed, if this were so? Surely people would either laugh at Him as unable to dispel disease or else consider Him lacking in proper human feeling because He could do so, but did not.

(23) Then, again, suppose without any illness He had just concealed His body somewhere, and then suddenly reappeared and said that He had risen from the dead. He would have been regarded merely as a teller of tales, and because there was no witness of His death, nobody would believe His resurrection. Death had to precede resurrection, for there could be no resurrection without it. A secret and unwitnessed death would have left the resurrection without any proof or evidence to support it. Again, why should He die a secret death, when He proclaimed the fact of His rising openly? Why should He drive out evil spirits and heal the man blind from birth and change water into wine, all publicly, in order to convince men that He was the Word, and not also declare publicly that incorruptibility of His mortal body, so that He might Himself be believed to be the Life? And how could His disciples have had boldness in speaking of the resurrection unless they could state it as a fact that He had first died? Or how could their hearers be expected to believe their assertion, unless they themselves also had witnessed His death? For if the Pharisees at the time refused to

believe and forced others to deny also, though the things had happened before their very eyes, how many excuses for unbelief would they have contrived, if it had taken place secretly? Or how could the end of death and the victory over it have been declared, had not the Lord thus challenged it before the sight of all, and by the incorruption of His body proved that henceforward it was annulled and void?

(24) There are some other possible objections that must be answered. Some might urge that, even granting the necessity of a public death for subsequent belief in the resurrection, it would surely have been better for Him to have arranged an honorable death for Himself, and so to have avoided the ignominy of the cross. But even this would have given ground for suspicion that His power over death was limited to the particular kind of death which He chose for Himself; and that again would furnish excuse for disbelieving the resurrection. Death came to His body, therefore, not from Himself but from enemy action, in order that the Savior might utterly abolish death in whatever form they offered it to Him. A generous wrestler, virile and strong, does not himself choose his antagonists, lest it should be thought that of some of them he is afraid. Rather, he lets the spectators choose them, and that all the more if these are hostile, so that he may overthrow whomsoever they match against him and thus vindicate his superior strength. Even so was it with Christ. He, the Life of all, our Lord and Savior, did not arrange the manner of his own death lest He should seem to be afraid of some other kind. No. He accepted and bore upon the cross a death inflicted by others, and those others His special enemies, a death which to them was supremely terrible and by no means to be faced; and He did this in order that, by destroying even this death, He might Himself be believed to be the Life, and the power of death be recognized as finally annulled. A marvelous and mighty paradox has thus occurred, for the death which they thought to inflict on Him as dishonor and disgrace has become the glorious monument to death's defeat. Therefore it is also, that He neither endured the death of John, who was beheaded, nor was He sawn asunder, like Isaiah: even in death He preserved His body whole and undivided, so that there should be no excuse hereafter for those who would divide the Church.

(25) So much for the objections of those outside the Church. But if any honest Christian wants to know why He suffered death on the cross and not in some other way, we answer thus: in no other way was it expedient for us, indeed the Lord offered for our sakes the one death

that was supremely good. He had come to bear the curse that lay on us; and how could He "become a curse" [27] otherwise than by accepting the accursed death? And that death is the cross, for it is written "Cursed is every one that hangeth on tree." [28] Again, the death of the Lord is the ransom of all, and by it "the middle wall of partition" [29] is broken down and the call of the Gentiles comes about. How could He have called us if He had not been crucified, for it is only on the cross that a man dies with arms outstretched? Here, again, we see the fitness of His death and of those outstretched arms: it was that He might draw His ancient people with the one and the Gentiles with the other, and join both together in Himself. Even so, He foretold the manner of His redeeming death, "I, if I be lifted up, will draw all men unto Myself." [30] Again, the air is the sphere of the devil, the enemy of our race who, having fallen from heaven, endeavors with the other evil spirits who shared in his disobedience both to keep souls from the truth and to hinder the progress of those who are trying to follow it. The apostle refers to this when he says, "According to the prince of the power of the air, of the spirit that now worketh in the sons of disobedience." [31] But the Lord came to overthrow the devil and to purify the air and to make "a way" for us up to heaven, as the apostle says, "through the veil, that is to say, His flesh." [32] This had to be done through death, and by what other kind of death could it be done, save by a death in the air, that is, on the cross? Here, again, you see how right and natural it was that the Lord should suffer thus; for being thus "lifted up," He cleansed the air from all the evil influences of the enemy. "I beheld Satan as lightning falling," [33] He says; and thus He re-opened the road to heaven, saying again, "Lift up your gates, O ye princes, and be ye lift up, ye everlasting doors." [34] For it was not the Word Himself Who needed an opening of the gates, He being Lord of all, nor was any of His works closed to their Maker. No, it was we who needed it, we whom He Himself upbore in His own body--that body which He first offered to death on behalf of all, and then made through it a path to heaven.

[25] Heb. ii. 14 f.
[26] 1 Cor. xv. 53 ff.
[27] Gal. iii. 13
[28] Gal. iii. 13
[29] Eph. ii. 14
[30] John xii. 32

[31] Eph. ii. 2
[32] Heb. x. 20
[33] Luke x. 18
[34] Psalm xxiv. 7

Chapter 5

The Resurrection

(26) Fitting indeed, then, and wholly consonant was the death on the cross for us; and we can see how reasonable it was, and why it is that the salvation of the world could be accomplished in no other way. Even on the cross He did not hide Himself from sight; rather, He made all creation witness to the presence of its Maker. Then, having once let it be seen that it was truly dead, He did not allow that temple of His body to linger long, but forthwith on the third day raised it up, impassable and incorruptible, the pledge and token of His victory.

It was, of course, within His power thus to have raised His body and displayed it as alive directly after death. But the all-wise Savior did not do this, lest some should deny that it had really or completely died. Besides this, had the interval between His death and resurrection been but two days, the glory of His incorruption might not have appeared. He waited one whole day to show that His body was really dead, and then on the third day showed it incorruptible to all. The interval was no longer, lest people should have forgotten about it and grown doubtful whether it were in truth the same body. No, while the affair was still ringing in their ears and their eyes were still straining and their minds in turmoil, and while those who had put Him to death were still on the spot and themselves witnessing to the fact of it, the Son of God after three days showed His once dead body immortal and incorruptible; and it was evident to all that it was from no natural weakness that the body which the Word indwelt had died, but in order that in it by the Savior's power death might be done away.

(27) A very strong proof of this destruction of death and its conquest by the cross is supplied by a present fact, namely this. All the disciples

of Christ despise death; they take the offensive against it and, instead of fearing it, by the sign of the cross and by faith in Christ trample on it as on something dead. Before the divine sojourn of the Savior, even the holiest of men were afraid of death, and mourned the dead as those who perish. But now that the Savior has raised His body, death is no longer terrible, but all those who believe in Christ tread it underfoot as nothing, and prefer to die rather than to deny their faith in Christ, knowing full well that when they die they do not perish, but live indeed, and become incorruptible through the resurrection. But that devil who of old wickedly exulted in death, now that the pains of death are loosed, he alone it is who remains truly dead. There is proof of this too; for men who, before they believe in Christ, think death horrible and are afraid of it, once they are converted despise it so completely that they go eagerly to meet it, and themselves become witnesses of the Savior's resurrection from it. Even children hasten thus to die, and not men only, but women train themselves by bodily discipline to meet it. So weak has death become that even women, who used to be taken in by it, mock at it now as a dead thing robbed of all its strength. Death has become like a tyrant who has been completely conquered by the legitimate monarch; bound hand and foot the passers-by sneer at him, hitting him and abusing him, no longer afraid of his cruelty and rage, because of the king who has conquered him. So has death been conquered and branded for what it is by the Savior on the cross. It is bound hand and foot, all who are in Christ trample it as they pass and as witnesses to Him deride it, scoffing and saying, "O Death, where is thy victory? O Grave, where is thy sting?" [35]

(28) Is this a slender proof of the impotence of death, do you think? Or is it a slight indication of the Savior's victory over it, when boys and young girls who are in Christ look beyond this present life and train themselves to die? Every one is by nature afraid of death and of bodily dissolution; the marvel of marvels is that he who is enfolded in the faith of the cross despises this natural fear and for the sake of the cross is no longer cowardly in face of it. The natural property of fire is to burn. Suppose, then, that there was a substance such as the Indian asbestos is said to be, which had no fear of being burnt, but rather displayed the impotence of the fire by proving itself unburnable. If anyone doubted the truth of this, all he need do would be to wrap himself up in the substance in question and then touch the fire. Or, again, to revert to our former figure, if anyone wanted to see the tyrant bound and helpless, who used to be such a terror to others, he could do so

simply by going into the country of the tyrant's conqueror. Even so, if anyone still doubts the conquest of death, after so many proofs and so many martyrdoms in Christ and such daily scorn of death by His truest servants, he certainly does well to marvel at so great a thing, but he must not be obstinate in unbelief and disregard of plain facts. No, he must be like the man who wants to prove the property of the asbestos, and like him who enters the conqueror's dominions to see the tyrant bound. He must embrace the faith of Christ, this disbeliever in the conquest of death, and come to His teaching. Then he will see how impotent death is and how completely conquered. Indeed, there have been many former unbelievers and deriders who, after they became believers, so scorned death as even themselves to become martyrs for Christ's sake.

(29) If, then, it is by the sign of the cross and by faith in Christ that death is trampled underfoot, it is clear that it is Christ Himself and none other Who is the Archvictor over death and has robbed it of its power. Death used to be strong and terrible, but now, since the sojourn of the Savior and the death and resurrection of His body, it is despised; and obviously it is by the very Christ Who mounted on the cross that it has been destroyed and vanquished finally. When the sun rises after the night and the whole world is lit up by it, nobody doubts that it is the sun which has thus shed its light everywhere and driven away the dark. Equally clear is it, since this utter scorning and trampling down of death has ensued upon the Savior's manifestation in the body and His death on the cross, that it is He Himself Who brought death to nought and daily raises monuments to His victory in His own disciples. How can you think otherwise, when you see men naturally weak hastening to death, unafraid at the prospect of corruption, fearless of the descent into Hades, even indeed with eager soul provoking it, not shrinking from tortures, but preferring thus to rush on death for Christ's sake, rather than to remain in this present life? If you see with your own eyes men and women and children, even, thus welcoming death for the sake of Christ's religion, how can you be so utterly silly and incredulous and maimed in your mind as not to realize that Christ, to Whom these all bear witness, Himself gives the victory to each, making death completely powerless for those who hold His faith and bear the sign of the cross? No one in his senses doubts that a snake is dead when he sees it trampled underfoot, especially when he knows how savage it used to be; nor, if he sees boys making fun of a lion, does he doubt that the brute is either dead or completely bereft of

strength. These things can be seen with our own eyes, and it is the same with the conquest of death. Doubt no longer, then, when you see death mocked and scorned by those who believe in Christ, that by Christ death was destroyed, and the corruption that goes with it resolved and brought to end.

(30) What we have said is, indeed, no small proof of the destruction of death and of the fact that the cross of the Lord is the monument to His victory. But the resurrection of the body to immortality, which results henceforward from the work of Christ, the common Savior and true Life of all, is more effectively proved by facts than by words to those whose mental vision is sound. For, if, as we have shown, death was destroyed and everybody tramples on it because of Christ, how much more did He Himself first trample and destroy it in His own body! Death having been slain by Him, then, what other issue could there be than the resurrection of His body and its open demonstration as the monument of His victory? How could the destruction of death have been manifested at all, had not the Lord's body been raised? But if anyone finds even this insufficient, let him find proof of what has been said in present facts. Dead men cannot take effective action; their power of influence on others lasts only till the grave. Deeds and actions that energize others belong only to the living. Well, then, look at the facts in this case. The Savior is working mightily among men, every day He is invisibly persuading numbers of people all over the world, both within and beyond the Greek-speaking world, to accept His faith and be obedient to His teaching. Can anyone, in face of this, still doubt that He has risen and lives, or rather that He is Himself the Life? Does a dead man prick the consciences of men, so that they throw all the traditions of their fathers to the winds and bow down before the teaching of Christ? If He is no longer active in the world, as He must needs be if He is dead, how is it that He makes the living to cease from their activities, the adulterer from his adultery, the murderer from murdering, the unjust from avarice, while the profane and godless man becomes religious? If He did not rise, but is still dead, how is it that He routs and persecutes and overthrows the false gods, whom unbelievers think to be alive, and the evil spirits whom they worship? For where Christ is named, idolatry is destroyed and the fraud of evil spirits is exposed; indeed, no such spirit can endure that Name, but takes to flight on sound of it. This is the work of One Who lives, not of one dead; and, more than that, it is the work of God. It would be absurd to say that the evil spirits whom He drives out and the

idols which He destroys are alive, but that He Who drives out and destroys, and Whom they themselves acknowledge to be Son of God, is dead.

(31) In a word, then, those who disbelieve in the resurrection have no support in facts, if their gods and evil spirits do not drive away the supposedly dead Christ. Rather, it is He Who convicts them of being dead. We are agreed that a dead person can do nothing: yet the Savior works mightily every day, drawing men to religion, persuading them to virtue, teaching them about immortality, quickening their thirst for heavenly things, revealing the knowledge of the Father, inspiring strength in face of death, manifesting Himself to each, and displacing the irreligion of idols; while the gods and evil spirits of the unbelievers can do none of these things, but rather become dead at Christ's presence, all their ostentation barren and void. By the sign of the cross, on the contrary, all magic is stayed, all sorcery confounded, all the idols are abandoned and deserted, and all senseless pleasure ceases, as the eye of faith looks up from earth to heaven. Whom, then, are we to call dead? Shall we call Christ dead, Who effects all this? But the dead have not the faculty to effect anything. Or shall we call death dead, which effects nothing whatever, but lies as lifeless and ineffective as are the evil spirits and the idols? The Son of God, "living and effective," [36] is active every day and effects the salvation of all; but death is daily proved to be stripped of all its strength, and it is the idols and the evil spirits who are dead, not He. No room for doubt remains, therefore, concerning the resurrection of His body.

Indeed, it would seem that he who disbelieves this bodily rising of the Lord is ignorant of the power of the Word and Wisdom of God. If He took a body to Himself at all, and made it His own in pursuance of His purpose, as we have shown that He did, what was the Lord to do with it, and what was ultimately to become of that body upon which the Word had descended? Mortal and offered to death on behalf of all as it was, it could not but die; indeed, it was for that very purpose that the Savior had prepared it for Himself. But on the other hand it could not remain dead, because it had become the very temple of Life. It therefore died, as mortal, but lived again because of the Life within it; and its resurrection is made known through its works.

(32) It is, indeed, in accordance with the nature of the invisible God that He should be thus known through His works; and those who doubt

the Lord's resurrection because they do not now behold Him with their eyes, might as well deny the very laws of nature. They have ground for disbelief when works are lacking; but when the works cry out and prove the fact so clearly, why do they deliberately deny the risen life so manifestly shown? Even if their mental faculties are defective, surely their eyes can give them irrefragable proof of the power and Godhead of Christ. A blind man cannot see the sun, but he knows that it is above the earth from the warmth which it affords; similarly, let those who are still in the blindness of unbelief recognize the Godhead of Christ and the resurrection which He has brought about through His manifested power in others. Obviously He would not be expelling evil spirits and despoiling idols, if He were dead, for the evil spirits would not obey one who was dead. If, on the other hand, the very naming of Him drives them forth, He clearly is not dead; and the more so that the spirits, who perceive things unseen by men, would know if He were so and would refuse to obey Him. But, as a matter of fact, what profane persons doubt, the evil spirits know--namely that He is God; and for that reason they flee from Him and fall at His feet, crying out even as they cried when He was in the body, "We know Thee Who Thou art, the Holy One of God," and, "Ah, what have I in common with Thee, Thou Son of God? I implore Thee, torment me not." [37]

Both from the confession of the evil spirits and from the daily witness of His works, it is manifest, then, and let none presume to doubt it, that the Savior has raised His own body, and that He is very Son of God, having His being from God as from a Father, Whose Word and Wisdom and Whose Power He is. He it is Who in these latter days assumed a body for the salvation of us all, and taught the world concerning the Father. He it is Who has destroyed death and freely graced us all with incorruption through the promise of the resurrection, having raised His own body as its first- fruits, and displayed it by the sign of the cross as the monument to His victory over death and its corruption.

[35] I Cor. xv. 55
[36] Heb. iv. 12
[37] Cf. Luke iv. 34 and Mark v. 7

Chapter 6

Refutation of the Jews

(33) We have dealt thus far with the Incarnation of our Savior, and have found clear proof of the resurrection of His Body and His victory over death. Let us now go further and investigate the unbelief and the ridicule with which Jews and Gentiles respectively regard these same facts. It seems that in both cases the points at issue are the same, namely the unfittingness or incongruity (as it seems to them) alike of the cross and of the Word's becoming man at all. But we have no hesitation in taking up the argument against these objectors, for the proofs on our side are extremely clear.

First, then, we will consider the Jews. Their unbelief has its refutation in the Scriptures which even themselves read; for from cover to cover the inspired Book clearly teaches these things both in its entirety and in its actual words. Prophets foretold the marvel of the Virgin and of the Birth from her, saying, "Behold, a virgin shall conceive and bear a son, and they shall call his name 'Emmanuel,' which means 'God is with us.'" [38] And Moses, that truly great one in whose word the Jews trust so implicitly, he also recognized the importance and truth of the matter. He puts it thus: "There shall arise a star from Jacob and a man from Israel, and he shall break in pieces the rulers of Moab. [39] And, again, "How lovely are thy dwellings, O Jacob, thy tents, O Israel! Like woodland valleys they give shade, and like parks by rivers, like tents which the Lord has pitched, like cedar-trees by streams. There shall come forth a Man from among his seed, and he shall rule over many peoples." [40] And, again, Isaiah says, "Before the Babe shall be old enough to call father or mother, he shall take the power of Damascus and the spoils of Samaria from under the eyes of the king of Assyria." [41] These words, then, foretell that a Man shall appear. And Scripture proclaims further that He that is to come is Lord of all. These are the words, "Behold, the Lord sitteth on an airy cloud and shall come into Egypt, and the man-made images of Egypt shall be shaken." [42] And it is from Egypt also that the Father calls him back, saying, "Out of Egypt have I called My Son." [43]

(34) Moreover, the Scriptures are not silent even about His death. On the contrary, they refer to it with the utmost clearness. They have not feared to speak also of the cause of it. He endures it, they say, not for His own sake, but for the sake of bringing immortality and salvation to all, and they record also the plotting of the Jews against Him and all the indignities which He suffered at their hands. Certainly nobody who reads the Scriptures can plead ignorance of the facts as an excuse for error! There is this passage, for instance: "A man that is afflicted and knows how to bear weakness, for His face is turned away. He was dishonored and not considered, He bears our sins and suffers for our sakes. And we for our part thought Him distressed and afflicted and ill-used; but it was for our sins that He was wounded and for our lawlessness that He was made weak. Chastisement for our peace was upon Him, and by His bruising we are healed." [44] O marvel at the love of the Word for men, for it is on our account that He is dishonored, so that we may be brought to honor. "For all we," it goes on, "have strayed like sheep, man has strayed from his path, and the Lord has given Him up for our sins; and He Himself did not open His mouth at the ill-treatment. Like a sheep He was led to slaughter, and as a lamb is dumb before its shearer, so He opened not His mouth; in His humiliation His judgment was taken away." [45] And then Scripture anticipates the surmises of any who might think from His suffering thus that He was just an ordinary man, and shows what power worked in His behalf. "Who shall declare of what lineage He comes?" it says, "for His life is exalted from the earth. By the lawlessnesses of the people was He brought to death, and I will give the wicked in return for His burial and the rich in return for His death. For He did no lawlessness, neither was deceit found in His mouth. And the Lord wills to heal Him of His affliction." [46]

(35) You have heard the prophecy of His death, and now, perhaps, you want to know what indications there are about the cross. Even this is not passed over in silence: on the contrary, the sacred writers proclaim it with the utmost plainness. Moses foretells it first, and that right loudly, when he says, "You shall see your Life hanging before your eyes, and shall not believe." [47] After him the prophets also give their

witness, saying, "But I as an innocent lamb brought to be offered was yet ignorant of it. They plotted evil against Me, saying, 'Come, let us cast wood into His bread, and wipe Him out from the land of the living." [48] And, again, "They pierced My hands and My feet, they counted all My bones, they divided My garments for themselves and cast lots for My clothing." [49] Now a death lifted up and that takes place on wood can be none other than the death of the cross; moreover, it is only in that death that the hands and feet are pierced. Besides this, since the Savior dwelt among men, all nations everywhere have begun to know God; and this too Holy Writ expressly mentions. "There shall be the Root of Jesse," it says, "and he who rises up to rule the nations, on Him nations shall set their hope." [50]

These are just a few things in proof of what has taken place; but indeed all Scripture teems with disproof of Jewish unbelief. For example, which of the righteous men and holy prophets and patriarchs of whom the Divine Scriptures tell ever had his bodily birth from a virgin only? Was not Abel born of Adam, Enoch of Jared, Noah of Lamech, Abraham of Terah, Isaac of Abraham, and Jacob of Isaac? Was not Judah begotten by Jacob and Moses and Aaron by Ameram? Was not Samuel the son of Elkanah, David of Jesse, Solomon of David, Hezekiah of Ahaz, Josiah of Amon, Isaiah of Amos, Jeremiah of Hilkiah and Ezekiel of Buzi? Had not each of these a father as author of his being? So who is He that is born of a virgin only, that sign of which the prophet makes so much? Again, which of all those people had his birth announced to the world by a star in the heavens? When Moses was born his parents hid him. David was unknown even in his own neighborhood, so that mighty Samuel himself was ignorant of his existence and asked whether Jesse had yet another son. Abraham again became known to his neighbors as a great man only after his birth. But with Christ it was otherwise. The witness to His birth was not man, but a star shining in the heavens whence He was coming down.

(36) Then, again, what king that ever was reigned and took trophies from his enemies before he had strength to call father or mother? Was not David thirty years old when he came to the throne and Solomon a grown young man? Did not Joash enter on his reign at the age of seven, and Josiah, some time after him, at about the same age, both of them fully able by that time to call father or mother? Who is there, then, that was reigning and despoiling his enemies almost before he was born? Let the Jews, who have investigated the matter, tell us if

there was ever such a king in Israel or Judah--a king upon whom all the nations set their hopes and had peace, instead of being at enmity with him on every side! As long as Jerusalem stood there was constant war between them, and they all fought against Israel. The Assyrians oppressed Israel, the Egyptians persecuted them, the Babylonians fell upon them, and, strange to relate, even the Syrians their neighbors were at war with them. And did not David fight with Moab and smite the Syrians, and Hezekiah quail at the boasting of Sennacherib? Did not Amalek make war on Moses and the Amorites oppose him, and did not the inhabitants of Jericho array themselves against Joshua the son of Nun? Did not the nations always regard Israel with implacable hostility? Then it is worth inquiring who it is, on whom the nations are to set their hopes. Obviously there must be someone, for the prophet could not have told a lie. But did any of the holy prophets or of the early patriarchs die on the cross for the salvation of all? Was any of them wounded and killed for the healing of all? Did the idols of Egypt fall down before any righteous man or king that came there? Abraham came there certainly, but idolatry prevailed just the same; and Moses was born there, but the mistaken worship was unchanged.

(37) Again, does Scripture tell of anyone who was pierced in hands and feet or hung upon a tree at all, and by means of a cross perfected his sacrifice for the salvation of all? It was not Abraham, for he died in his bed, as did also Isaac and Jacob. Moses and Aaron died in the mountain, and David ended his days in his house, without anybody having plotted against him. Certainly he had been sought by Saul, but he was preserved unharmed. Again Isaiah was sawn asunder, but he was not hung on a tree. Jeremiah was shamefully used, but he did not die under condemnation. Ezekiel suffered, but he did so, not on behalf of the people, but only to signify to them what was going to happen. Moreover, all these even when they suffered were but men, like other men; but He Whom the Scriptures declare to suffer on behalf of all is called not merely man but Life of all, although in point of fact He did share our human nature. "You shall see your Life hanging before your eyes," they say, and "Who shall declare of what lineage He comes?" With all the saints we can trace their descent from the beginning, and see exactly how each came to be; but the Divine Word maintains that we cannot declare the lineage of Him Who is the Life. Who is it, then, of Whom Holy Writ thus speaks? Who is there so great that even the prophets foretell of Him such mighty things? There is indeed no one in the Scriptures at all, save the common Savior of all, the Word of God,

our Lord Jesus Christ. He it is that proceeded from a virgin, and appeared as man on earth, He it is Whose earthly lineage cannot be declared, because He alone derives His body from no human father, but from a virgin alone. We can trace the paternal descent of David and Moses and of all the patriarchs. But with the Savior we cannot do so, for it was He Himself Who caused the star to announce His bodily birth, and it was fitting that the Word, when He came down from heaven, should have His sign in heaven too, and fitting that the King of creation on His coming forth should be visibly recognized by all the world. He was actually born in Judea, yet men from Persia came to worship Him. He it is Who won victory from His demon foes and trophies from the idolaters even before His bodily appearing--namely, all the heathen who from every region have abjured the tradition of their fathers and the false worship of idols and are now placing their hope in Christ and transferring their allegiance to Him. The thing is happening before our very eyes, here in Egypt; and thereby another prophecy is fulfilled, for at no other time have the Egyptians ceased from their false worship save when the Lord of all, riding as on a cloud, came down here in the body and brought the error of idols to nothing and won over everybody to Himself and through Himself to the Father. He it is Who was crucified with the sun and moon as witnesses; and by His death salvation has come to all men, and all creation has been redeemed. He is the Life of all, and He it is Who like a sheep gave up His own body to death, His life for ours and our salvation.

(38) Yet the Jews disbelieve this. This argument does not satisfy them. Well, then, let them be persuaded by other things in their own oracles. Of whom, for instance, do the prophets say "I was made manifest to those who did not seek Me, I was found by those who had not asked for Me? I said, 'See, here am I,' to the nation that had not called upon My Name. I stretched out My hands to a disobedient and gainsaying people." [51] Who is this person that was made manifest, one might ask the Jews? If the prophet is speaking of himself, then they must tell us how he was first hidden, in order to be manifested afterwards. And, again, what kind of man is this prophet, who was not only revealed after being hidden, but also stretched out his hands upon the cross? Those things happened to none of those righteous men: they happened only to the Word of God Who, being by nature without body, on our account appeared in a body and suffered for us all. And if even this is not enough for them, there is other overwhelming evidence by which they may be silenced. The Scripture says, "Be strong, hands that hang

down and feeble knees, take courage, you of little faith, be strong and do not fear. See, our God will recompense judgment, He Himself will come and save us. Then the eyes of blind men shall be opened and the ears of deaf men shall hear, and stammerers shall speak distinctly." [52] What can they say to this, or how can they look it in the face at all? For the prophecy does not only declare that God will dwell here, it also makes known the signs and the time of His coming. When God comes, it says, the blind will see, the lame will walk, the deaf will hear and the stammerers will speak distinctly. Can the Jews tell us when such signs occurred in Israel, or when anything of the kind took place at all in Jewry? The leper Naaman was cleansed, it is true, but no deaf man heard nor did any lame man walk. Elijah raised a dead person and so did Elisha; but no one blind from birth received his sight. To raise a dead person is a great thing indeed, but it is not such as the Savior did. And surely, since the Scriptures have not kept silence about the leper and the dead son of the widow, if a lame man had walked and a blind man had received his sight, they would have mentioned these as well. Their silence on these points proves that the events never took place. When therefore did these things happen, unless when the Word of God Himself came in the body? Was it not when He came that lame men walked and stammerers spoke clearly and men blind from birth were given sight? And the Jews who saw it themselves testified to the fact that such things had never before occurred. "Since the world began," they said, "it has never been heard of that anyone should open the eyes of a man born blind. If this Man were not from God, He could do nothing." [53]

(39) But surely they cannot fight against plain facts. So it may be that, without denying what is written, they will maintain that they are still waiting for these things to happen, and that the Word of God is yet to come, for that is a theme on which they are always harping most brazenly, in spite of all the evidence against them. But they shall be refuted on this supreme point more clearly than on any, and that not by ourselves but by the most wise Daniel, for he signifies the actual date of the Savior's coming as well as His Divine sojourn in our midst. "Seventy weeks," he says, "are cut short upon thy people and upon the holy city, to make a complete end of sin and for sins to be sealed up and iniquities blotted out, and to make reconciliation for iniquity and to seal vision and prophet, and to anoint a Holy One of holies. And thou shalt know and understand from the going forth of the Word to answer, [54] and to build Jerusalem, until Christ the Prince." [55] In re-

gard to the other prophecies, they may possibly be able to find excuses for deferring their reference to a future time, but what can they say to this one? How can they face it at all? Not only does it expressly mention the Anointed One, that is the Christ, it even declares that He Who is to be anointed is not man only, but the Holy One of holies! And it says that Jerusalem is to stand till His coming, and that after it prophet and vision shall cease in Israel! David was anointed of old, and Solomon, and Hezekiah; but then Jerusalem and the place stood, and prophets were prophesying, Gad and Asaph and Nathan, and later Isaiah and Hosea and Amos and others. Moreover, those men who were anointed were called holy certainly, but none of them was called the Holy of holies. Nor is it any use for the Jews to take refuge in the Captivity, and say that Jerusalem did not exist then, for what about the prophets? It is a fact that at the outset of the Exile Daniel and Jeremiah were there, and Ezekiel and Haggai and Zechariah also prophesied.

(40) So the Jews are indulging in fiction, and transferring present time to future. When did prophet and vision cease from Israel? Was it not when Christ came, the Holy One of holies? It is, in fact, a sign and notable proof of the coming of the Word that Jerusalem no longer stands, neither is prophet raised up nor vision revealed among them. And it is natural that it should be so, for when He that was signified had come, what need was there any longer of any to signify Him? And when the Truth had come, what further need was there of the shadow? On His account only they prophesied continually, until such time as Essential Righteousness has come, Who was made the Ransom for the sins of all. For the same reason Jerusalem stood until the same time, in order that there men might premeditate the types before the Truth was known. So, of course, once the Holy One of holies had come, both vision and prophecy were sealed. And the kingdom of Jerusalem ceased at the same time, because kings were to be anointed among them only until the Holy of holies had been anointed. Moses also prophesies that the kingdom of the Jews shall stand until His time, saying, "A ruler shall not fail from Judah nor a prince from his loins, until the things laid up for him shall come and the Expectation of the nations Himself." [56] And that is why the Savior Himself was always proclaiming "The law and the prophets prophesied until John." [57] So if there is still king or prophet or vision among the Jews, they do well to deny that Christ is come; but if there is neither king nor vision, and since that time all prophecy has been sealed and city and temple taken, how can they be so irreligious, how can they so flaunt the facts, as to

deny Christ Who has brought it all about? Again, they see the heathen forsaking idols and setting their hopes through Christ on the God of Israel; why do they yet deny Christ Who after the flesh was born of the root of Jesse and reigns henceforward? Of course, if the heathen were worshipping some other god, and not confessing the God of Abraham and Isaac and Jacob and Moses, then they would do well to argue that God had not come. But if the heathen are honoring the same God Who gave the law to Moses and the promises to Abraham--the God Whose word too the Jews dishonored, why do they not recognize or rather why do they deliberately refuse to see that the Lord of Whom the Scriptures prophesied has shone forth to the world and appeared to it in a bodily form? Scripture declares it repeatedly. "The Lord God has appeared to us," [58] and again, "He sent forth His Word and healed them." [59] And again, "It was no ambassador, no angel who saved us, but the Lord Himself." [60] The Jews are afflicted like some demented person who sees the earth lit up by the sun, but denies the sun that lights it up! What more is there for their Expected One to do when he comes? To call the heathen? But they are called already. To put an end to prophet and king and vision? But this too has already happened. To expose the Goddenyingness of idols? It is already exposed and condemned. Or to destroy death? It is already destroyed. What then has not come to pass that the Christ must do? What is there left out or unfulfilled that the Jews should disbelieve so light-heartedly? The plain fact is, as I say, that there is no longer any king or prophet nor Jerusalem nor sacrifice nor vision among them; yet the whole earth is filled with the knowledge of God, and the Gentiles, forsaking atheism, are now taking refuge with the God of Abraham through the Word, our Lord Jesus Christ.

Surely, then, it must be plain even to the most shameless that the Christ has come, and that He has enlightened all men everywhere, and given them the true and divine teaching about His Father.

Thus the Jews may be refuted by these and other arguments from the Divine teaching.

[38] Isaiah vii. 14
[39] Numbers xxiv. 17
[40] Numbers xxiv. 5-7
[41] Isaiah viii. 4

[42] Isaiah xix. 1
[43] Hosea xi. 1
[44] Isaiah liii. 3-5
[45] Isaiah liii. 6-8
[46] Isaiah liii. 8-10
[47] Deut. xxviii. 66
[48] Jer. xi. 19
[49] Psalm xxii. 16-18
[50] Isaiah xi. 10
[51] Isaiah lxv. 1, 2
[52] Isaiah xxxv. 3-6
[53] John ix. 32, 33
[54] "Answer" is LXX misreading for Hebrew "restore."
[55] Daniel ix. 24, 25
[56] Gen. xlix. 10
[57] Matt. xi. 13
[58] Psalm cxviii. 27
[59] Psalm cvii. 20
[60] Isaiah lxiii. 9

Chapter 7

Refutation of the Gentiles

(41) We come now to the unbelief of the Gentiles; and this is indeed a matter for complete astonishment, for they laugh at that which is no fit subject for mockery, yet fail to see the shame and ridiculousness of their own idols. But the arguments on our side do not lack weight, so we will confute them too on reasonable grounds, chiefly from what we ourselves also see.

First of all, what is there in our belief that is unfitting or ridiculous? Is it only that we say that the Word has been manifested in a body? Well, if they themselves really love the truth, they will agree with us that this involved no unfittingness at all. If they deny that there is a Word of God at all, that will be extraordinary, for then they will be ridiculing what they do not know. But suppose they confess that there is a Word of God, that He is the Governor of all things, that in Elim the Father wrought the creation, that by His providence the whole receives light and life and being, and that He is King over all, so that He is known by means of the works of His providence, and through Him the Father. Suppose they confess all this, what then? Are they not unknowingly turning the ridicule against themselves? The Greek philosophers say that the universe is a great body, and they say truly, for we perceive the universe and its parts with our senses. But if the Word of God is in the universe, which is a body, and has entered into it in its every part, what is there surprising or unfitting in our saying that He has entered also into human nature? If it were unfitting for Him to have embodied Himself at all, then it would be unfitting for Him to have entered into the universe, and to be giving light and movement by His providence to all things in it, because the universe, as we have seen, is itself a body. But if it is right and fitting for Him to enter into the universe and to reveal Himself through it, then, because humanity is part of the universe along with the rest, it is no less fitting for Him to appear in a human body, and to enlighten and to work through that. And surely if it were wrong for a part of the universe to have been used to reveal His Divinity to men, it would be much more wrong that He should be so revealed by the whole!

(42) Take a parallel case. A man's personality actuates and quickens his whole body. If anyone said it was unsuitable for the man's power to be in the toe, he would be thought silly, because, while granting that a man penetrates and actuates the whole of his body, he denied his presence in the part. Similarly, no one who admits the presence of the Word of God in the universe as a whole should think it unsuitable for a single human body to be by Him actuated and enlightened.

But is it, perhaps, because humanity is a thing created and brought into being out of non-existence that they regard as unfitting the manifestation of the Savior in our nature? If so, it is high time that they spurned Him from creation too; for it, too, has been brought out of non-being into being by the Word. But if, on the other hand, although creation is a thing that has been made, it is not unsuitable for the Word to be present in it, then neither is it unsuitable for Him to be in man. Man is a part of the creation, as I said before; and the reasoning which applies to one applies to the other. All things derive from the Word their light and movement and life, as the Gentile authors themselves say, "In Him we live and move and have our being." [61] Very well then. That being so, it is by no means unbecoming that the Word should dwell in man. So if, as we say, the Word has used that in which He is as the means of His self-manifestation, what is there ridiculous in that? He could not have used it had He not been present in it; but we have already admitted that He is present both in the whole and in the parts. What, then, is there incredible in His manifesting Himself through that in which He is? By His own power He enters completely into each and all, and orders them throughout ungrudgingly; and, had He so willed, He could have revealed Himself and His Father by means of sun or moon or sky or earth or fire or water. Had He done so, no one could rightly have accused Him of acting unbecomingly, for He sustains in one whole all things at once, being present and invisibly revealed not only in the whole, but also in each particular part. This being so, and since, moreover, He has willed to reveal Himself through men, who are part of the whole, there can be nothing ridiculous in His using a human body to manifest the truth and knowledge of the Father. Does not the mind of man pervade his entire being, and yet find expression through one part only, namely the tongue? Does anybody say on that account that Mind has degraded itself? Of course not. Very well, then, no more is it degrading for the Word, Who pervades all things, to have appeared in a human body. For, as I said before, if it were unfitting for Him thus to indwell the part, it would be equally so for Him to exist within the whole.

(43) Some may then ask, why did He not manifest Himself by means of other and nobler parts of creation, and use some nobler instrument, such as sun or moon or stars or fire or air, instead of mere man? The answer is this. The Lord did not come to make a display. He came to heal and to teach suffering men. For one who wanted to make a display the thing would have been just to appear and dazzle the beholders. But for Him Who came to heal and to teach the way was not merely to dwell here, but to put Himself at the disposal of those who needed Him, and to be manifested according as they could bear it, not vitiating the value of the Divine appearing by exceeding their capacity to receive it.

Moreover, nothing in creation had erred from the path of God's purpose for it, save only man. Sun, moon, heaven, stars, water, air, none of these had swerved from their order, but, knowing the Word as their Maker and their King, remained as they were made. Men alone having rejected what is good, have invented nothings instead of the truth, and have ascribed the honor due to God and the knowledge concerning Him to demons and men in the form of stones. Obviously the Divine goodness could not overlook so grave a matter as this. But men could not recognize Him as ordering and ruling creation as a whole. So what does He do? He takes to Himself for instrument a part of the whole, namely a human body, and enters into that. Thus He ensured that men should recognize Him in the part who could not do so in the whole, and that those who could not lift their eyes to His unseen power might recognize and behold Him in the likeness of themselves. For, being men, they would naturally learn to know His Father more quickly and directly by means of a body that corresponded to their own and by the Divine works done through it; for by comparing His works with their own they would judge His to be not human but Divine. And if, as they say, it were unsuitable for the Word to reveal Himself through bodily acts, it would be equally so for Him to do so through the works of the universe. His being in creation does not mean that He shares its nature; on the contrary, all created things partake of His power. Similarly, though He used the body as His instrument, He shared nothing of its defect, [62] but rather sanctified it by His indwelling. Does not even Plato, of whom the Greeks think so much, say that the Author of the Universe, seeing it storm-tossed and in danger of sinking into the state of dissolution, takes his seat at the helm of the Life-force of the universe, and comes to the rescue and puts everything right? What, then, is there incredible in our saying that, mankind having gone astray, the Word descended upon it and was manifest as man, so that by His intrinsic goodness and His steersmanship He might save it from the storm?

(44) It may be, however, that, though shamed into agreeing that this objection is void, the Greeks will want to raise another. They will say that, if God wanted to instruct and save mankind, He might have done so, not by His Word's assumption of a body, but, even as He at first created them, by the mere signification of His will. The reasonable reply to that is that the circumstances in the two cases are quite different. In the beginning, nothing as yet existed at all; all that was needed, therefore, in order to bring all things into being, was that His will to do so should be signified. But once man was in existence, and things that were, not things that were not, demanded to be healed, it followed as a matter of course that the Healer and Savior should align Himself with those things that existed already, in order to heal the existing evil. For that reason, therefore, He was made man, and used the body as His human instrument. If this were not the fitting way, and He willed to use an instrument at all, how otherwise was the Word to come? And whence could He take His instrument, save from among those already in existence and needing His Godhead through One like themselves? It was not things non-existent that needed salvation, for which a bare creative word might have sufficed, but man--man already in existence and already in process of corruption and ruin. It was natural and right, therefore, for the Word to use a human instrument and by that means unfold Himself to all.

You must know, moreover, that the corruption which had set in was not external to the body but established within it. The need, therefore, was that life should cleave to it in corruption's place, so that, just as death was brought into being in the body, life also might be engendered in it. If death had been exterior to the body, life might fittingly have been the same. But if death was within the body, woven into its very substance and dominating it as though completely one with it, the need was for Life to be woven into it instead, so that the body by thus enduing itself with life might cast corruption off. Suppose the Word had come outside the body instead of in it, He would, of course, have defeated death, because death is powerless against the Life. But the corruption inherent in the body would have remained in it none the less. Naturally, therefore, the Savior assumed a body for Himself, in order that the body, being interwoven as it were with life, should no longer remain a mortal thing, in thrall to death, but as endued with immortality and risen from death, should thenceforth remain immortal. For once having put op corruption, it could not rise, unless it put on life instead; and besides this, death of its very nature could not appear otherwise than in a body. Therefore He put on a body, so that in the body He might find death and blot it out. And, indeed, how could the Lord have been proved to be the Life at all, had He not endued with life that which was subject to death? Take an illustration. Stubble is a substance naturally destructible by fire; and it still remains stubble, fearing the menace of fire which has the natural property of consuming it, even if fire is kept away from it, so that it is not actually burnt. But suppose that, instead of merely keeping the fire from it somebody soaks the stubble with a quantity of asbestos, the substance which is said to be the antidote to fire. Then the stubble no longer fears the fire, because it has put on that which fire cannot touch, and therefore it is safe. It is just the same with regard to the body and death. Had death been kept from it by a mere command, it would still have remained mortal and corruptible, according to its nature. To prevent this, it put on the incorporeal Word of God, and therefore fears neither death nor corruption any more, for it is clad with Life as with a garment and in it corruption is clean done away.

(45) The Word of God thus acted consistently in assuming a body and using a human instrument to vitalize the body. He was consistent in working through man to reveal Himself everywhere, as well as through the other parts of His creation, so that nothing was left void of His Divinity and knowledge. For I take up now the point I made before, namely that the Savior did this in order that He might fill all things everywhere with the knowledge of Himself, just as they are already filled with His presence, even as the Divine Scripture says, "The whole universe was filled with the knowledge of the Lord." [63] If a man looks up to heaven he sees there His ordering; but if he cannot

look so high as heaven, but only so far as men, through His works he sees His power, incomparable with human might, and learns from them that He alone among men is God the Word. Or, if a man has gone astray among demons and is in fear of them, he may see this Man drive them out and judge therefrom that He is indeed their Master. Again, if a man has been immersed in the element of water and thinks that it is God--as indeed the Egyptians do worship water--he may see its very nature changed by Him and learn that the Lord is Creator of all. And if a man has gone down even to Hades, and stands awestruck before the heroes who have descended thither, regarding them as gods, still he may see the fact of Christ's resurrection and His victory over death, and reason from it that, of all these, He alone is very Lord and God.

For the Lord touched all parts of creation, and freed and undeceived them all from every deceit. As St. Paul says, "Having put off from Himself the principalities and the powers, He triumphed on the cross," [64] so that no one could possibly be any longer deceived, but everywhere might find the very Word of God. For thus man, enclosed on every side by the works of creation and everywhere--in heaven, in Hades, in men and on the earth, beholding the unfolded Godhead of the Word, is no longer deceived concerning God, but worships Christ alone, and through Him rightly knows the Father.

On these grounds, then, of reason and of principle, we will fairly silence the Gentiles in their turn. But if they think these arguments insufficient to confute them, we will go on in the next chapter to prove our point from facts.

[61] See Acts xvii. 28
[62] Literally, "He shared nothing of the things of the body."
[63] Isaiah xi. 9
[64] Col. ii. 15

Chapter 8

Refutation of the Gentiles--continued

(46) When did people begin to abandon the worship of idols, unless it were since the very Word of God came among men? When have oracles ceased and become void of meaning, among the Greeks and everywhere, except since the Savior has revealed Himself on earth? When did those whom the poets call gods and heroes begin to be adjudged as mere mortals, except when the Lord took the spoils of death and preserved incorruptible the body He had taken, raising it from among the dead? Or when did the deceitfulness and madness of demons fall under contempt, save when the Word, the Power of God, the Master of all these as well, condescended on account of the weakness of mankind and appeared on earth? When did the practice and theory of magic begin to be spurned under foot, if not at the manifestation of the Divine Word to men? In a word, when did the wisdom of the Greeks become foolish, save when the true Wisdom of God revealed Himself on earth? In old times the whole world and every place in it was led astray by the worship of idols, and men thought the idols were the only gods that were. But now all over the world men are forsaking the fear of idols and taking refuge with Christ; and by worshipping Him as God they come through Him to know the Father also, Whom formerly they did not know. The amazing thing, moreover, is this. The objects of worship formerly were varied and countless; each place had its own idol and the so-called god of one place could not pass over to another in order to persuade the people there to worship him, but was barely reverenced even by his own. Indeed no! Nobody worshipped his neighbor's god, but every man had his own idol and thought that it was lord of all. But now Christ alone is worshipped, as One and the Same among all peoples everywhere; and what the feebleness of idols could not do, namely, convince even those dwelling close at hand, He has effected. He has persuaded not only those close at hand, but liter-

ally the entire world to worship one and the same Lord and through Him the Father.

(47) Again, in former times every place was full of the fraud of the oracles, and the utterances of those at Delphi and Dordona and in Boeotia and Lycia and Libya and Egypt and those of the Kabiri and the Pythoness were considered marvelous by the minds of men. But now, since Christ has been proclaimed everywhere, their madness too has ceased, and there is no one left among them to give oracles at all. Then, too, demons used to deceive men's minds by taking up their abode in springs or rivers or trees or stones and imposing upon simple people by their frauds. But now, since the Divine appearing of the Word, all this fantasy has ceased, for by the sign of the cross, if a man will but use it, he drives out their deceits. Again, people used to regard as gods those who are mentioned in the poets--Zeus and Kronos and Apollo and the heroes, and in worshipping them they went astray. But now that the Savior has appeared among men, those others have been exposed as mortal men, and Christ alone is recognized as true God, Word of God, God Himself. And what is one to say about the magic that they think so marvelous? Before the sojourn of the Word, it was strong and active among Egyptians and Chaldeans and Indians and filled all who saw it with terror and astonishment. But by the coming of the Truth and the manifestation of the Word it too has been confuted and entirely destroyed. As to Greek wisdom, however, and the philosophers' noisy talk, I really think no one requires argument from us; for the amazing fact is patent to all that, for all that they had written so much, the Greeks failed to convince even a few from their own neighborhood in regard to immortality and the virtuous ordering of life. Christ alone, using common speech and through the agency of men not clever with their tongues, has convinced whole assemblies of people all the world over to despise death, and to take heed to the things that do not die, to look past the things of time and gaze on things eternal, to think nothing of earthly glory and to aspire only to immortality.

(48) These things which we have said are no mere words: they are attested by actual experience. Anyone who likes may see the proof of glory in the virgins of Christ, and in the young men who practice chastity as part of their religion, and in the assurance of immortality in so great and glad a company [65] of martyrs. Anyone, too, may put what we have said to the proof of experience in another way. In the very

presence of the fraud of demons and the imposture of the oracles and the wonders of magic, let him use the sign of the cross which they all mock at, and but speak the Name of Christ, and he shall see how through Him demons are routed, oracles cease, and all magic and witchcraft is confounded.

Who, then, is this Christ and how great is He, Who by His Name and presence overshadows and confounds all things on every side, Who alone is strong against all and has filled the whole world with His teaching? Let the Greeks tell us, who mock at Him without stint or shame. If He is a man, how is it that one man has proved stronger than all those whom they themselves regard as gods, and by His own power has shown them to be nothing? If they call Him a magician, how is it that by a magician all magic is destroyed, instead of being rendered strong? Had He conquered certain magicians or proved Himself superior to one of them only, they might reasonably think that He excelled the rest only by His greater skill. But the fact is that His cross has vanquished all magic entirely and has conquered the very name of it. Obviously, therefore, the Savior is no magician, for the very demons whom the magicians invoke flee from Him as from their Master. Who is He, then? Let the Greeks tell us, whose only serious pursuit is mockery! Perhaps they will say that He, too, is a demon, and that is why He prevailed. But even so the laugh is still on our side. for we can confute them by the same proofs as before. How could He be a demon, Who drives demons out? If it were only certain ones that He drove out, then they might reasonably think that He prevailed against them through the power of their Chief, as the Jews, wishing to insult Him, actually said. But since the fact is, here again, that at the mere naming of His Name all madness of the demons is rooted out and put to flight, obviously the Greeks are wrong here, too, and our Lord and Savior Christ is not, as they maintain, some demonic power.

If, then, the Savior is neither a mere man nor a magician, nor one of the demons, but has by His Godhead confounded and overshadowed the opinions of the poets and the delusion of the demons and the wisdom of the Greeks, it must be manifest and will be owned by all that He is in truth Son of God, Existent Word and Wisdom and Power of the Father. This is the reason why His works are no mere human works, but, both intrinsically and by comparison with those of men, are recognized as being superhuman and truly the works of God.

(49) What man that ever was, for instance, formed a body for himself from a virgin only? Or what man ever healed so many diseases as the common Lord of all? Who restored that which was lacking in man's nature or made one blind from birth to see? Aesculapius was deified by the Greeks because he practiced the art of healing and discovered herbs as remedies for bodily diseases, not, of course, forming them himself out of the earth, but finding them out by the study of nature. But what is that in comparison with what the Savior did when, instead of just healing a wound, He both fashioned essential being and restored to health the thing that He had formed? Hercules, too, is worshipped as a god by the Greeks because he fought against other men and destroyed wild animals by craft. But what is that to what the Word did, in driving away from men diseases and demons and even death itself? Dionysus is worshipped among them, because he taught men drunkenness; yet they ridicule the true Savior and Lord of all, Who taught men temperance.

That, however, is enough on this point. What will they say to the other marvels of His Godhead? At what man's death was the sun darkened and the earth shaken? Why, even to this day men are dying, and they did so also before that time. When did any such marvels happen in their case? Now shall we pass over the deeds done in His earthly body and mention those after His resurrection? Has any man's teaching, in any place or at any time, ever prevailed everywhere as one and the same, from one end of the earth to the other, so that his worship has fairly flown through every land? Again, if, as they say, Christ is man only and not God the Word, why do not the gods of the Greeks prevent His entering their domains? Or why, on the other hand, does the Word Himself dwelling in our midst make an end of their worship by His teaching and put their fraud to shame?

(50) Many before Him have been kings and tyrants of the earth, history tells also of many among the Chaldeans and Egyptians and Indians who were wise men and magicians. But which of those, I do not say after his death, but while yet in this life, was ever able so far to prevail as to fill the whole world with his teaching and retrieve so great a multitude from the craven fear of idols, as our Savior has won over from idols to Himself? The Greek philosophers have compiled many works with persuasiveness and much skill in words; but what fruit have they to show for this such as has the cross of Christ? Their

wise thoughts were persuasive enough until they died; yet even in their life-time their seeming influence was counterbalanced by their rivalry with one another, for they were a jealous company and declaimed against each other. But the Word of God, by strangest paradox, teaching in meaner language, has put the choicest sophists in the shade, and by confounding their teachings and drawing all men to Himself He has filled His own assemblies. Moreover, and this is the marvelous thing by going down as Man to death He has confounded ail the sounding utterances of the wise men about the idols. For whose death ever drove out demons, or whose death did ever demons fear, save that of Christ? For where the Savior is named, there every demon is driven out. Again, who has ever so rid men of their natural passions that fornicators become chaste and murderers no longer wield the sword and those who formerly were craven cowards boldly play the man? In a word, what persuaded the barbarians and heathen folk in every place to drop their madness and give heed to peace, save the faith of Christ and the sign of the cross? What other things have given men such certain faith in immortality as have the cross of Christ and the resurrection of His body? The Greeks told all sorts of false tales, but they could never pretend that their idols rose again from death: indeed it never entered their heads that a body could exist again after death at all. And one would be particularly ready to listen to them on this point, because by these opinions they have exposed the weakness of their own idolatry, at the same time yielding to Christ the possibility of bodily resurrection, so that by that means He might be recognized by all as Son of God.

(51) Again, who among men, either after his death or while yet living, taught about virginity and did not account this virtue impossible for human beings? But Christ our Savior and King of all has so prevailed with His teaching on this subject that even children not yet of lawful age promise that virginity which transcends the law. And who among men has ever been able to penetrate even to Scythians and Ethiopians, or Parthians or Armenians or those who are said to live beyond Hyrcania, or even the Egyptians and Chaldeans, people who give heed to magic and are more than naturally enslaved by the fear of demons and savage in their habits, and to preach at all about virtue and self-control and against the worshipping of idols, as has the Lord of all, the Power of God, our Lord Jesus Christ? Yet He not only preached through His own disciples, but also wrought so persuasively on men's understanding that, laying aside their savage habits and forsaking the worship of their ancestral gods, they learnt to know Him and through Him to wor-

ship the Father. While they were yet idolaters, the Greeks and Barbarians were always at war with each other, and were even cruel to their own kith and kin. Nobody could travel by land or sea at all unless he was armed with swords, because of their irreconcilable quarrels with each other. Indeed, the whole course of their life was carried on with the weapons, and the sword with them replaced the staff and was the mainstay of all aid. All this time, as I said before, they were serving idols and offering sacrifices to demons, and for all the superstitious awe that accompanied this idol worship, nothing could wean them from that warlike spirit. But, strange to relate, since they came over to the school of Christ, as men moved with real compunction they have laid aside their murderous cruelty and are war-minded no more. On the contrary, all is peace among them and nothing remains save desire for friendship.

(52) Who, then, is He Who has done these things and has united in peace those who hated each other, save the beloved Son of the Father, the common Savior of all, Jesus Christ, Who by His own love underwent all things for our salvation? Even from the beginning, moreover, this peace that He was to administer was foretold, for Scripture says, "They shall beat their swords into ploughshares and their spears into sickles, and nation shall not take sword against nation, neither shall they learn any more to wage war." [66] Nor is this by any means incredible.

The barbarians of the present day are naturally savage in their habits, and as long as they sacrifice to their idols they rage furiously against each other and cannot bear to be a single hour without weapons. But when they hear the teaching of Christ, forthwith they turn from fighting to farming, and instead of arming themselves with swords extend their hands in prayer. In a word, instead of fighting each other, they take up arms against the devil and the demons, and overcome them by their selfcommand and integrity of soul. These facts are proof of the Godhead of the Savior, for He has taught men what they could never learn among the idols. It is also no small exposure of the weakness and nothingness of demons and idols, for it was because they knew their own weakness that the demons were always setting men to fight each other, fearing lest, if they ceased from mutual strife, they would turn to attack the demons themselves. For in truth the disciples of Christ, instead of fighting each other, stand arrayed against demons by their habits and virtuous actions, and chase them away and mock at their captain the devil. Even in youth they are chaste, they endure in times of testing and persevere in toils. When they are insulted, they are patient, when robbed they make light of it, and, marvelous to relate, they make light even of death itself, and become martyrs of Christ.

(53) And here is another proof of the Godhead of the Savior, which is indeed utterly amazing. What mere man or magician or tyrant or king was ever able by himself to do so much? Did anyone ever fight against the whole system of idol-worship and the whole host of demons and all magic and all the wisdom of the Greeks, at a time when all of these were strong and flourishing and taking everybody in, as did our Lord, the very Word of God? Yet He is even now invisibly exposing every man's error, and single-handed is carrying off all men from them all, so that those who used to worship idols now tread them under foot, reputed magicians burn their books and the wise prefer to all studies the interpretation of the gospels. They are deserting those whom formerly they worshipped, they worship and confess as Christ and God Him Whom they used to ridicule as crucified. Their so-called gods are routed by the sign of the cross, and the crucified Savior is proclaimed in all the world as God and Son of God. Moreover, the gods worshipped among the Greeks are now falling into disrepute among them on account of the disgraceful things they did, for those who receive the teaching of Christ are more chaste in life than they. If these, and the like of them, are human works, let anyone who will show us similar ones done by men in former time, and so convince us. But if they are shown to be, and are the works not of men but of God, why are the unbelievers so irreligious as not to recognize the Master Who did them? They are afflicted as a man would be who failed to recognize God the Artificer through the works of creation. For surely if they had recognized His Godhead through His power over the universe, they would recognize also that the bodily works of Christ are not human, but are those of the Savior of all, the Word of God. And had they recognized this, as Paul says, "They would not have crucified the Lord of glory." [67]

(54) As, then, he who desires to see God Who by nature is invisible and not to be beheld, may yet perceive and know Him through His

works, so too let him who does not see Christ with his understanding at least consider Him in His bodily works and test whether they be of man or God. If they be of man, then let him scoff; but if they be of God, let him not mock at things which are no fit subject for scorn, but rather let him recognize the fact and marvel that things divine have been revealed to us by such humble means, that through death deathlessness has been made known to us, and through the Incarnation of the Word the Mind whence all things proceed has been declared, and its Agent and Ordainer, the Word of God Himself. He, indeed, assumed humanity that we might become God. He manifested Himself by means of a body in order that we might perceive the Mind of the unseen Father. He endured shame from men that we might inherit immortality. He Himself was unhurt by this, for He is impassable and incorruptible; but by His own impassability He kept and healed the suffering men on whose account He thus endured. In short, such and so many are the Savior's achievements that follow from His Incarnation, that to try to number them is like gazing at the open sea and trying to count the waves. One cannot see all the waves with one's eyes, for when one tries to do so those that are following on baffle one's senses. Even so, when one wants to take in all the achievements of Christ in the body, one cannot do so, even by reckoning them up, for the things that transcend one's thought are always more than those one thinks that one has grasped.

As we cannot speak adequately about even a part of His work, therefore, it will be better for us not to speak about it as a whole. So we will mention but one thing more, and then leave the whole for you to marvel at. For, indeed, everything about it is marvelous, and wherever a man turns his gaze he sees the Godhead of the Word and is smitten with awe.

(55) The substance of what we have said so far may be summarized as follows. Since the Savior came to dwell among us, not only does idolatry no longer increase, but it is getting less and gradually ceasing to be. Similarly, not only does the wisdom of the Greeks no longer make any progress, but that which used to be is disappearing. And demons, so far from continuing to impose on people by their deceits and oracle-givings and sorceries, are routed by the sign of the cross if they so much as try. On the other hand, while idolatry and everything

else that opposes the faith of Christ is daily dwindling and weakening and falling, see, the Savior's teaching is increasing everywhere! Worship, then, the Savior "Who is above all" and mighty, even God the Word, and condemn those who are being defeated and made to disappear by Him. When the sun has come, darkness prevails no longer; any of it that may be left anywhere is driven away. So also, now that the Divine epiphany of the Word of God has taken place, the darkness of idols prevails no more, and all parts of the world in every direction are enlightened by His teaching. Similarly, if a king be reigning somewhere, but stays in his own house and does not let himself be seen, it often happens that some insubordinate fellows, taking advantage of his retirement, will have themselves proclaimed in his stead; and each of them, being invested with the semblance of kingship, misleads the simple who, because they cannot enter the palace and see the real king, are led astray by just hearing a king named. When the real king emerges, however, and appears to view, things stand differently. The insubordinate impostors are shown up by his presence, and men, seeing the real king, forsake those who previously misled them. In the same way the demons used formerly to impose on men, investing themselves with the honor due to God. But since the Word of God has been manifested in a body, and has made known to us His own Father, the fraud of the demons is stopped and made to disappear; and men, turning their eyes to the true God, Word of the Father, forsake the idols and come to know the true God.

Now this is proof that Christ is God, the Word and Power of God. For whereas human things cease and the fact of Christ remains, it is clear to all that the things which cease are temporary, but that He Who remains is God and very Son of God, the sole-begotten Word.

[65] Literally, "so great a chorus . . .". "choros" being properly a band of dancers and singers.
[66] Isaiah ii. 4
[67] Cor. ii. 8

Chapter 9

Conclusion

(56) Here, then, Macarius, is our offering to you who love Christ, a brief statement of the faith of Christ and of the manifestation of His Godhead to us. This will give you a beginning, and you must go on to prove its truth by the study of the Scriptures. They were written and inspired by God; and we, who have learned from inspired teachers who read the Scriptures and became martyrs for the Godhead of Christ, make further contribution to your eagerness to learn. From the Scriptures you will learn also of His second manifestation to us, glorious and divine indeed, when He shall come not in lowliness but in His proper glory, no longer in humiliation but in majesty, no longer to suffer but to bestow on us all the fruit of His cross--the resurrection and incorruptibility. No longer will He then be judged, but rather will Himself be Judge, judging each and all according to their deeds done in the body, whether good or ill. Then for the good is laid up the heavenly kingdom, but for those that practice evil outer darkness and the eternal fire. So also the Lord Himself says, "I say unto you, hereafter ye shall see the Son of Man seated on the right hand of power, coming on the clouds of heaven in the glory of the Father." [68] For that Day we have one of His own sayings to prepare us, "Get ready and watch, for ye know not the hour in which He cometh" [69] And blessed Paul says, "We must all stand before the judgment seat of Christ, that each one may receive according as he practiced in the body, whether good or ill." [70]

(57) But for the searching and right understanding of the Scriptures there is need of a good life and a pure soul, and for Christian virtue to guide the mind to grasp, so far as human nature can, the truth concern-

ing God the Word. One cannot possibly understand the teaching of the saints unless one has a pure mind and is trying to imitate their life. Anyone who wants to look at sunlight naturally wipes his eye clear first, in order to make, at any rate, some approximation to the purity of that on which he looks; and a person wishing to see a city or country goes to the place in order to do so. Similarly, anyone who wishes to understand the mind of the sacred writers must first cleanse his own life, and approach the saints by copying their deeds. Thus united to them in the fellowship of life, he will both understand the things revealed to them by God and, thenceforth escaping the peril that threatens sinners in the judgment, will receive that which is laid up for the saints in the kingdom of heaven. Of that reward it is written: "Eye hath not seen nor ear heard, neither hath entered into the heart of man the things that God has prepared" [71] for them that live a godly life and love the God and Father in Christ Jesus our Lord, through Whom and with Whom be to the Father Himself, with the Son Himself, in the Holy Spirit, honor and might and glory to ages of ages. Amen.

[68] Matt.xxvi. 64
[69] Matt. xxiv. 42
[70] 2 Cor. v. 10
[71] 1 Cor. ii. 9

Index of Scripture References

Genesis
[1]1:1   [2]2:6   [3]49:10
Numbers
[4]24:5-7   [5]24:17
Deuteronomy
[6]28:66
Psalms
[7]22:16-18   [8]24:7   [9]82:6   [10]107:20   [11]118:27
Isaiah
[12]2:4   [13]7:14   [14]8:4   [15]11:9   [16]11:10   [17]19:1 [18]35:3-6   [19]53:3-5   [20]53:6-8   [21]53:8-10   [22]63:9 [23]65:1-2
Jeremiah
[24]11:19
Daniel
[25]9:24-25
Hosea
[26]11:1
Matthew
[27]11:13   [28]19:4-6   [29]24:42   [30]26:64
Mark
[31]5:7
Luke
[32]4:34   [33]10:18   [34]19:10   [35]19:10
John
[36]1:3   [37]3:3   [38]9:32-33   [39]10:37-38   [40]12:32
Acts
[41]17:28
Romans
[42]1:25   [43]1:26
1 Corinthians [44]1:21   [45]2:9   [46]15:21   [47]15:53   [48]15:55
2 Corinthians [49]5:10   [50]5:14

Galatians [51]3:13   [52]3:13
Ephesians [53]2:2   [54]2:14   [55]3:17
Colossians [56]2:15
1 Timothy [57]6:15
Hebrews [58]2:9   [59]2:14   [60]2:14   [61]4:12   [62]10:20   [63]11:3
Wisdom of Solomon [64]2:23   [65]6:18

Against the Heathen

§1

Introduction:--The purpose of the book a vindication of Christian doctrine, and especially of the Cross, against the scoffing objection of Gentiles. The effects of this doctrine its main vindication.

The knowledge of our religion and of the truth of things is independently manifest rather than in need of human teachers, for almost day by day it asserts itself by facts, and manifests itself brighter than the sun by the doctrine of Christ. 2. Still, as you nevertheless desire to hear about it, Macarius [101] , come let us as we may be able set forth a few points of the faith of Christ: able though you are to find it out from the divine oracles, but yet generously desiring to hear from others as well. 3. For although the sacred and inspired Scriptures are sufficient [102] to declare the truth,--while there are other works of our blessed teachers [103] compiled for this purpose, if he meet with which a man will gain some knowledge of the interpretation of the Scriptures, and be able to learn what he wishes to know,--still, as we have not at present in our hands the compositions of our teachers, we must communicate in writing to you what we learned from them,--the faith, namely, of Christ the Saviour; lest any should hold cheap the doctrine taught among us, or think faith. in Christ unreasonable. For this is what the Gentiles traduce and scoff at, and laugh loudly at us, insisting on the one fact of the Cross of Christ; and it is just here that one must pity their want of sense, because when they traduce the Cross of Christ they do not see that its power has filled all the world, and that by it the effects of the knowledge of God are made manifest to all. 4. For they would not have scoffed at such a fact, had they, too, been men who genuinely gave heed to His divine Nature. On the contrary, they in their turn would have recognised this man as Saviour of the world, and that the Cross has been not a disaster, but a healing of Creation. 5. For if after the Cross all idolatry was overthrown, while every manifestation of demons is driven away by this Sign [104] , and Christ alone is worshipped and the Father known through Him, and, while gainsayers are put to shame, He daily invisibly wins over the souls of these gain-sayers [105] ,--how, one might fairly ask them, is it still open to us to regard the matter as human, instead of confessing that He Who ascended the Cross is Word of God and Saviour of the World? But these men seem to me quite as bad as one who should traduce the sun when covered by clouds, while yet wondering at his light, seeing how the whole of creation is illumined by him. 6. For as the light is noble, and the sun, the chief cause of light, is nobler still, so, as it is a divine thing for the whole world to be filled with his knowledge, it follows that the orderer and chief cause of such an achievement is God and the Word of God. 7. We speak then as lies within our power, first refuting the ignorance of the unbelieving; so that what is false being refuted, the truth may then shine forth of itself, and that you yourself, friend, may be reassured that you have believed what is true, and in coming to know Christ have not been deceived. Moreover, I think it becoming to discourse to you, as a lover of Christ, about Christ, since I am sure that you rate faith in and knowledge of Him above anything else whatsoever.

[101] See de Incarn. 1 and note there.
[102] Constantly insisted on by Athan. Cf. de Incarn. 5, and note on de Decr. 32.
[103] De Incarn. 56. 2; he may also be referring to works from the Alex. school, such as Orig. de Princ.
[104] Cf. de Incarn. 47. 2, 48. 3, Vit. Ant. passim.
[105] Cf. de Incarn. 50. 3, 51. 3, &c.

§2

Evil no part of the essential nature of things. The original creation and constitution of man in grace and in the knowledge of God.

In the beginning wickedness did not exist. Nor indeed does it exist even now in those who are holy, nor does it in any way belong to their nature. But men later on began to contrive it and to elaborate it to their own hurt. Whence also they devised the invention of idols, treating what was not as though it were. 2. For God Maker of all and King of all, that has His Being beyond [106] all substance and human discovery, inasmuch as He is good and exceeding noble, made, through His own Word our Saviour Jesus Christ, the human race after His own image, and constituted man able to see and know realities by means of this assimilation to Himself, giving him also a conception [107] and knowledge even of His own eternity, in order that, preserving his nature intact, he might not ever either depart from his idea of God, nor recoil from the communion of the holy ones; but having the grace of Him that gave it, having also God's own power from the Word of the Father, he might rejoice and have fellowship with the Deity, living the life of immortality unharmed and truly blessed. For having nothing to hinder his knowledge of the Deity, he ever beholds, by his purity, the Image of the Father, God the Word, after Whose image he himself is made. He is awe-struck as he contemplates that Providence [108] which through the Word extends to the universe, being raised above the things of sense and every bodily appearance, but cleaving to the divine and thought-perceived things in the heavens by the power of his mind. 3. For when the mind of men does not hold converse with bodies, nor has mingled with it from without aught of their lust, but is wholly above them, dwelling with itself as it was made to begin with, then, transcending the things of sense and all things human, it is raised up on high; and seeing the Word, it sees in Him also the Father of the Word, taking pleasure in contemplating Him, and gaining renewal by its desire toward Him; 4. exactly as the first of men created, the one who was named Adam in Hebrew, is described in the Holy Scriptures as having at the beginning had his mind to God-ward in a freedom un-embarrassed by shame, and as associating with the holy ones in that contemplation of things perceived by the mind which he enjoyed in the place where he was--the place which the holy Moses called in figure a Garden. So purity of soul is sufficient of itself to reflect God, as the Lord also says, "Blessed are the pure in heart, for they shall see God."

[106] See Orig. c. Cels. vii. 42 sqq. de Princ. I. 1.
[107] Restored in Christ, see §34.
[108] Cf. Ep. Æg. 15, Apol. Fug. passim, Orat. iii. 37.

§3

The decline of man from the above condition, owing to his absorption in material things.

Thus then, as we have said, the Creator fashioned the race of men, and thus meant it to remain. But men, making light of better things, and holding back from apprehending them, began to seek in preference things nearer to themselves. 2. But nearer to themselves were the body and its senses; so that while removing their mind from the things perceived by thought, they began to regard themselves; and so doing, and holding to the body and the other things of sense, and deceived as it were in their own surroundings, they fell into lust of themselves, preferring what was their own to the contemplation of what belonged to God. Having then made themselves at home in these things, and not being willing to leave what was so near to them, they entangled their soul with bodily pleasures, vexed and turbid with all kind of lusts, while they wholly forgot the power they originally had from God. 3. But the truth of this one may see from the man who was first made, according to what the holy Scriptures tell us of him. For he also, as long as he kept his mind to God, and the contemplation of God, turned away from the contemplation of the body. But when, by counsel of the serpent, he departed from the consideration of God, and began to regard himself, then they not only fell to bodily lust, but knew that they were naked, and knowing, were ashamed. But they knew that they were naked, not so much of clothing as that they were become stripped of the contemplation of divine things, and had transferred their understanding to the contraries. For having departed from the consideration of the one and the true, namely, God, and from desire of Him, they had thenceforward embarked in divers lusts and in those of the several bodily senses. 4. Next, as is apt to happen, having formed a desire for each and sundry, they began to be habituated to these desires, so that they were even afraid to leave them: whence the soul became subject to cowardice and alarms, and pleasures and thoughts of mortality. For not being willing to leave her lusts, she fears death and her separation from the body. But again, from lusting, and not meeting with gratification, she learned to commit murder and wrong. We are then led naturally to shew, as best we can, how she does this.

§4

The gradual abasement of the Soul from Truth to Falsehood by the abuse of her freedom of Choice.

Having departed from the contemplation of the things of thought, and using to the full the several activities of the body, and being pleased with the contemplation of the body, and seeing that pleasure is good for her, she was misled and abused the name of good, and thought that pleasure was the very essence of good: just as though a man out of his mind and asking for a sword to use against all he met, were to think that soundness of mind. 2. But having fallen in love with pleasure, she began to work it out in various ways. For being by nature mobile, even though she have turned away from what is good, yet she does not lose her mobility. She moves then, no longer according to virtue or so as to see God, but imagining false things, she makes a novel use of her power, abusing it as a means to the pleasures she has devised, since she is after all made with power over herself. 3. For she is able, as on the one hand to incline to what is good, so on the other to reject it; but in rejecting the good she of course entertains the thought of what is opposed to it, for she cannot at all cease from movement, being, as I said before, mobile by nature. And knowing her own power over herself, she sees that she is able to use the members of her body in either direction, both toward what is, or toward what is not. 4. But good is, while evil is not; by what is, then, I mean what is good, inasmuch as it has its pattern in God Who is. But by what is not I mean what is evil, in so far as it consists in a false imagination in the thoughts of men. For though the body has eyes so as to see Creation, and by its entirely harmonious construction to recognise the Creator; and ears to listen to the divine oracles and the laws of God; and hands both to perform works of necessity and to raise to God in prayer; yet the soul, departing from the contemplation of what is good and from moving in its sphere, wanders away and moves toward its contraries.

5. Then seeing, as I said before, and abusing her power, she has perceived that she can move the members of the body also in an opposite way: and so, instead of beholding the Creation, she turns the eye to lusts, shewing that she has this power too; and thinking that by the mere fact of moving she is maintaining her own dignity, and is doing no sin in doing as she pleases; not knowing that she is made not merely to move, but to move in the right direction. For this is why an apostolic utterance assures us "All things are lawful, but not all things are expedient [109] ."

[109] 1 Cor. x. 23.

§5

Evil, then consists essentially in the choice of what is lower in preference to what is higher.

But the audacity of men, having regard not to what is expedient and becoming, but to what is possible for it, began to do the contrary; whence, moving their hands to the contrary, it made them commit murder, and led away their hearing to disobedience, and their other members to adultery instead of to lawful procreation; and the tongue, instead of right speaking, to slander and insult and perjury; the hands again, to stealing and striking fellow-men; and the sense of smell to many sorts of lascivious odours; the feet, to be swift to shed blood, and the belly to drunkenness and insatiable gluttony [110] . 2. All of which things are a vice and sin of the soul: neither is there any cause of them at all, but only the rejection of better things. For just as if a charioteer [111] , having mounted his chariot on the race-course, were to pay no attention to the goal, toward which he should be driving, but, ignoring this, simply were to drive the horse as he could, or in other words as he would, and often drive against those he met, and often down steep places, rushing wherever he impelled himself by the speed of the team, thinking that thus running he has not missed the goal,--for he regards the running only, and does not see that he has passed wide of the goal;--so the soul too, turning from the way toward God, and driving the members of the body beyond what is proper, or rather, driven herself along with them by her own doing, sins and makes mischief for herself, not seeing that she has strayed from the way, and has swerved from the goal of truth, to which the Christ-bearing man, the blessed Paul, was looking when he said, "I press on toward the goal unto the prize of the high calling of Christ Jesus [112] :" so that the holy man, making the good his mark, never did what was evil.

[110] Rom. iii. 10 foll.
[111] Cf. Plato Phædrus 246 C, 248 A, 253 E, 254.
[112] Phil. iii. 14.

§6

False views of the nature of evil: viz., that evil is something in the nature of things, and has substantive existence. (a) Heathen thinkers: (evil resides in matter). Their refutation. (b) Heretical teachers: (Dualism). Refutation from Scripture.

Now certain of the Greeks, having erred from the right way, and not having known Christ, have ascribed to evil a substantive and independent existence. In this they make a double mistake: either in denying the Creator to be maker of all things, if evil had an independent subsistence and being of its own; or again, if they mean that He is maker of all things, they will of necessity admit Him to be maker of evil also. For evil, according to them, is included among existing things. 2. But this must appear paradoxical and impossible. For evil does not come from good, nor is it in, or the result of, good, since in that case it would not be good, being mixed in its nature or a cause of evil. 3. But the sectaries, who have fallen away from the teaching of the Church, and made shipwreck concerning the Faith [113], they also wrongly think that evil has a substantive existence. But they arbitrarily imagine another god besides the true One, the Father of our Lord Jesus Christ, and that he is the unmade producer of evil and the head of wickedness, who is also artificer of Creation. But these men one can easily refute, not only from the divine Scriptures, but also from the human understanding itself, the very source of these their insane imaginations. 4. To begin with, our Lord and Saviour Jesus Christ says in His own gospels confirming the words of Moses: "The Lord God is one;" and "I thank thee, Father, Lord of heaven and earth [114] ." But if God is one, and at the same time Lord of heaven and earth, how could there be another God beside Him? or what room will there be for the God whom they suppose, if the one true God fills all things in the compass of heaven and earth? or how could there be another creator of that, whereof, according to the Saviour's utterance, the God and Father of Christ is Himself Lord. 5. Unless indeed they would say that it were, so to speak, in an equipoise, and the evil god capable of getting the better of the good God. But if they say this, see to what a pitch of impiety they descend. For when powers are equal, the superior and better cannot be discovered. For if the one exist even if the other will it not, both are equally strong and equally weak equally, because the very existence of either is a defeat of the other's will: weak, because what happens is counter to their wills: for while the good God exists in spite of the evil one, the evil god exists equally in spite of the good.

[113] 1 Tim. i. 19.
[114] Mark xii. 29; Matt. xi. 25.

§7

Refutation of dualism from reason. Impossibility of two Gods.
The truth as to evil is that which the Church teaches: that it
originates, and resides, in the perverted choice of the darkened
soul.

More especially, they are exposed to the following reply. If visible things are the work of the evil god, what is the work of the good God? for nothing is to be seen except the work of the Artificer. Or what evidence is there that the good God exists at all, if there are no works of His by which He may be known? for by his works the artificer is known. 2. Or how could two principles exist, contrary one to another: or what is it that divides them, for them to exist apart? For it is impossible for them to exist together, because they are mutually destructive. But neither can the one be included in the other, their nature being unmixed and unlike. Accordingly that which divides them will evidently be of a third nature, and itself God. But of what nature could this third something be? good or evil? It will be impossible to determine, for it cannot be of the nature of both. 3. This conceit of theirs, then, being evidently rotten, the truth of the Church's theology must be manifest: that evil has not from the beginning been with God or in God, nor has any substantive existence; but that men, in default of the vision of good, began to devise and imagine for themselves what was not, after their own pleasure. 4. For as if a man, when the sun is shining, and the whole earth illumined by his light, were to shut fast his eyes and imagine darkness where no darkness exists, and then walk wandering as if in darkness, often falling and going down steep places, thinking it was dark and not light,--for, imagining that he sees, he does not see at all;--so, too, the soul of man, shutting fast her eyes, by which she is able to see God, has imagined evil for herself, and moving therein, knows not that, thinking she is doing something, she is doing nothing. For she is imagining what is not, nor is she abiding in her original nature; but what she is is evidently the product of her own disorder. 5. For she is made to see God, and to be enlightened by Him; but of her own accord in God's stead she has sought corruptible things and darkness, as the Spirit says somewhere in writing, "God made man upright, but they have sought out many inventions [115] ." Thus it has been then that men from the first discovered and contrived and imagined evil for themselves. But it is now time to say how they came down to the madness of idolatry, that you may know that the invention of idols is wholly due, not to good but to evil. But what has its origin in evil can never be pronounced good in any point,--being evil altogether.

[115] Eccl. vii. 29.

§8

The origin of idolatry is similar. The soul, materialised by forgetting God, and engrossed in earthly things, makes them into gods. The race of men descends into a hopeless depth of delusion and superstition.

Now the soul of mankind, not satisfied with the devising of evil, began by degrees to venture upon what is worse still. For having experience of diversities of pleasures, and girt about with oblivion of things divine; being pleased moreover and having in view the passions of the body, and nothing but things present and opinions about them, ceased to think that anything existed beyond what is seen, or that anything was good save things temporal and bodily; so turning away and forgetting that she was in the image of the good God, she no longer, by the power which is in her, sees God the Word after whose likeness she is made; but having departed from herself, imagines and feigns what is not. 2. For hiding, by the complications of bodily lusts, the mirror which, as it were, is in her, by which alone she had the power of seeing the Image of the Father, she no longer sees what a soul ought to behold, but is carried about by everything, and only sees the things which come under the senses. Hence, weighted with all fleshly desire, and distracted among the impressions of these things, she imagines that the God Whom her understanding has forgotten is to be found in bodily and sensible things, giving to things seen the name of God, and glorifying only those things which she desires and which are pleasant to her eyes. 3. Accordingly, evil is the cause which brings idolatry in its train; for men, having learned to contrive evil, which is no reality in itself, in like manner feigned for themselves as gods beings that had no real existence. Just, then, as though a man had plunged into the deep, and no longer saw the light, nor what appears by light, because his eyes are turned downwards, and the water is all above him; and, perceiving only the things in the deep, thinks that nothing exists beside them, but that the things he sees are the only true realities; so the men of former time, having lost their reason, and plunged into the lusts and imaginations of carnal things, and forgotten the knowledge and glory of God, their reasoning being dull, or rather following unreason, made gods for themselves of things seen, glorifying the creature rather than the Creator [116] , and deifying the works rather than the Master, God, their Cause and Artificer. 4. But just as, according to the above simile, men who plunge into the deep, the deeper they go down, advance into darker and deeper places, so it is with mankind. For they did not keep to idolatry in a simple form, nor did they abide in that with which they began; but the longer they went on in their first condition, the more new superstitions they invented: and, not satiated with the first evils, they again filled themselves. with others, advancing further in utter shamefulness, and surpassing themselves in impiety. But to this the divine Scripture testifies when it says, "When the wicked cometh unto the depth of evils, he despiseth [117] ."

[116] Rom. i. 25.
[117] Prov. xviii. 3.

§9

The various developments of idolatry: worship of the heavenly bodies, the elements, natural objects, fabulous creatures, personified lusts, men living and dead. The case of Antinous, and of the deified Emperors.

For now the understanding of mankind leaped asunder from God; and going lower in their ideas and imaginations, they gave the honour due to God first to the heaven and the sun and moon and the stars, thinking them to be not only gods, but also the causes of the other gods lower than themselves [118] . Then, going yet lower in their dark imaginations, they gave the name of gods to the upper æther and the air and the things in the air. Next, advancing further in evil, they came to celebrate as gods the elements and the principles of which bodies are composed, heat and cold and dryness and wetness. 2. But just as they who have fallen flat creep in the slime like land-snails, so the most impious of mankind, having fallen lower and lower from the idea of God, then set up as gods men, and the forms of men, some still living, others even after their death. Moreover, counselling and imagining worse things still, they transferred the divine and supernatural name of God at last even to stones and stocks, and creeping things both of land and water, and irrational wild beasts, awarding to them every divine honour, and turning from the true and only real God, the Father of Christ. 3. But would that even there the audacity of these foolish men had stopped short, and that they had not gone further yet in impious self-confusion. For to such a depth have some fallen in their understanding, to such darkness of mind, that they have even devised for themselves, and made gods of things that have no existence at all, nor any place among things created. For mixing up the rational with the irrational, and combining things unlike in nature, they worship the result as gods, such as the dog-headed and snake-headed and ass-headed gods among the Egyptians, and the ram-headed Ammon among the Libyans. While others, dividing apart the portions of men's bodies, head, shoulder, hand, and foot, have set up each as gods and deified them, as though their religion were not satisfied with the whole body in its integrity. 4. But others, straining impiety to the utmost, have deified the motive of the invention of these things and of their own wickedness, namely, pleasure and lust, and worship them, such as their Eros, and the Aphrodite at Paphos. While some of them, as if vying with them in depravation, have ventured to erect into gods their rulers or even their sons, either out of honour for their princes, or from fear of their tyranny, such as the Cretan Zeus, of such renown among them, and the Arcadian Hermes; and among the Indians Dionysus, among the Egyptians Isis and Osiris and Horus, and in our own time Antinous, favourite of Hadrian, Emperor of the Romans, whom, although men know he was a mere man, and not a respectable man, but on the contrary, full of licentiousness, yet they worship for fear of him that enjoined it. For Hadrian having come to sojourn in the land of Egypt, when Antinous the minister of his pleasure died, ordered him to be worshipped; being indeed himself in love with the youth even after his death, but for all that offering a convincing exposure of himself, and a proof against all idolatry, that it was discovered among men for no other reason than by reason of the lust of them that imagined it. According as the wisdom of God testifies beforehand when it says, "The devising of idols was the beginning of fornication [119] ." 5. And do not wonder, nor think what we are saying hard to believe, inasmuch as it is not long since, even if it be not still the case that the Roman Senate vote to those emperors who have ever ruled them from the beginning, either all of them, or such as they wish and decide, a place among the gods, and decree them to be worshipped [120] . For those to whom they are hostile, they treat as enemies and call men, admitting their real nature, while those who are popular with them they order to be worshipped on account of their virtue, as though they had it in their own power to make gods, though they are themselves men, and do not profess to be other than mortal. 6. Whereas if they are to make gods, they ought to be themselves gods; for that which makes must needs be better than that which it makes, and he that judges is of necessity in authority over him that is judged, while he that gives, at any rate that which he has, confers a layout, just as, of course, every king, in giving as a favour what he has to give, is greater and in a higher position than those who receive. If then they decree whomsoever they please to be gods, they ought first to be gods themselves. But the strange thing is this, that they themselves by dying as men, expose the falsehood of their own vote concerning those deified by them.

[118] For the following chapters Döllinger, The Gentile and the Jew,', is a rich mine of illustration. The recently published Manual of the History of Religions,' by Prof. Chantepie de la Saussaye (Eng. Tra. pub. by Longmans), summarises the best results of recent research.
[119] Wisd. xiv. 12.
[120] Constantine was the last Emperor officially deified (D.C.B., I. 649), but even Theodosius is raised to heaven by the courtly Claudian Carm. de 111 Cons. Honor. 163 sqq.; cf. Gwatkin, p. 54, note.

<h1 align="center">§10</h1>

. Similar human origin of the Greek gods, by decree of Theseus.
The process by which mortals became deified.

But this custom is not a new one, nor did it begin from the Roman Senate: on the contrary, it had existed previously from of old, and was formerly practised for the devising of idols. For the gods renowned from of old among the Greeks, Zeus, Poseidon, Apollo, Hephæstus, Hermes, and, among females, Hera and Demeter and Athena and Artemis, were decreed the title of gods by the order of Theseus, of whom Greek history tells us [121] ; and so the men who pass such decrees die like men and are mourned for, while those in whose favour they are passed are worshipped as gods. What a height of inconsistency and madness! knowing who passed the decree, they pay greater honour to those who are the subjects of it. 2. And would that their idolatrous madness had stopped short at males, and that they had not brought down the title of deity to females. For even women, whom it is not safe to admit to deliberation about public affairs, they worship and serve with the honour due to God, such as those enjoined by Theseus as above stated, and among the Egyptians [122] Isis and the Maid and the Younger one [123] , and among others Aphrodite. For the names of the others I do not consider it modest even to mention, full as they are of all kind of grotesqueness. 3. For many, not only in ancient times but in our own also, having lost their beloved ones, brothers and kinsfolk and wives; and many women who had lost their husbands, all of whom nature proved to be mortal men, made representations of them and devised sacrifices, and consecrated them; while later ages, moved by the figure and the brilliancy of the artist, worshipped them as gods, thus falling into inconsistency with nature [124] . For whereas their parents had mourned for them, not regarding them as gods (for had they known them to be gods they would not have lamented them as if they had perished; for this was why they represented them in an image, namely, because they not only did not think them gods, but did not believe them to exist at all, and in order that the sight of their form in the image might console them for their being no more), yet the foolish people pray to them as gods and invest them with the honour of the true God. 4. For example, in Egypt, even to this day, the death-dirge is celebrated for Osiris and Horus and Typho and the others. And the caldrons [125] at Dodona, and the Corybantes in Crete, prove that Zeus is no god but a man, and a man born of a cannibal father. And, strange to say, even Plato, the sage admired among the Greeks, with all his vaunted understanding about God, goes down with Socrates to Peiræus [126] to worship Artemis, a figment of man's art.

[121] This is probably a reference to the hiera anagraphe of Euhemerus, which Christian apologists commonly took as genuine history: see §12, note 1.

[122] Cf. de la Saussaye, §51. Isis, as goddess of the earth, corresponded to Demeter; as goddess of the dead, to the Kore (Persephone).

[123] The Neotera is a puzzle. The most likely suggestion is that of Montfaucon, who refers it to Cleopatra, who nea Isis echrematize (Plut. Vit. Anton.). He cites also a coin of M. Antony, on which Cleopatra is figured as thea neotera. Several such are given by Vaillant, de Numism. Cleopatr. 189. She was not the first of her name to adopt this style, see Head Hist. Num. pp. 716, 717. The text might be rendered Isis, both the Maid and the Younger.'

[124] Cf. Wisd. xiv. 12 sqq. quoted below.

[125] Cf. Greg. Naz. Or. v. 32, p. 168 c, and Dict. G. and R. Geog. I. p. 783a.

[126] Plat. Rep. I. ad init.

§11

The deeds of heathen deities, and particularly of Zeus.

But of these and such like inventions of idolatrous madness, Scripture taught us beforehand long ago, when it said [127] , "The devising of idols was the beginning of fornication, and the invention of them, the corruption of life. For neither were they from the beginning, neither shall they be for ever. For the vainglory of men they entered into the world, and therefore shall they come shortly to an end. For a father afflicted with untimely mourning when he hath made an image of his child soon taken away, now honoured him as a god which was then a dead man, and delivered to those that were under him ceremonies and sacrifices. Thus in process of time an ungodly custom grown strong was kept as a law. And graven images were worshipped by the commands of kings. Whom men could not honour in presence because they dwelt afar off, they took the counterfeit of his visage from afar, and made an express image of the king whom they honoured, to the end that by this their forwardness they might flatter him that was absent as if he were present. Also the singular diligence of the artificer did help to set forward the ignorant to more superstition: for he, peradventure, willing to please one in authority, forced all his skill to make the resemblance of the best fashion: and so the multitude, allured by the grace of the work, took him now for a god, which a little before was but honoured as a man: and this was an occasion to deceive the world, for men serving either calamity or tyranny, did ascribe unto stones and stocks the incommunicable Name." 2. The beginning and devising of the invention of idols having been, as Scripture witnesses, of such sort, it is now time to shew thee the refutation of it by proofs derived not so much from without as from these men's own opinions about the idols. For to begin at the lowest point, if one were to take the actions of them they call gods, one would find that they were not only no gods, but had been even of men the most contemptible. For what a thing it is to see the loves and licentious actions of Zeus in the poets! What a thing to hear of him, on the one hand carrying off Ganymede and committing stealthy adulteries, on the other in panic and alarm lest the walls of the Trojans should be destroyed against his intentions! What a thing to see him in grief at the death of his son Sarpedon, and wishing to succour him without being able to do so, and, when plotted against by the other so-called gods, namely, Athena and Hera and Poseidon, succoured by Thetis, a woman, and by Ægaeon of the hundred hands, and overcome by pleasures, a slave to women, and for their sakes running adventures in disguises consisting of brute beasts and creeping things and birds; and again, in hiding on account of his father's designs upon him, or Cronos bound by him, or him again mutilating his father! Why, is it fitting to regard as a god one who has perpetrated such deeds, and who stands accused of things which not even the public laws of the Romans allow those to do who are merely men?

[127] Wisd. xiv. 12 sqq.

§12.

Other shameful actions ascribed to heathen deities. All prove
that they are but men of former times, and not even good men.

For, to mention a few instances out of many to avoid prolix-
ity, who that saw his lawless and corrupt conduct toward Semele,
Leda, Alcmene, Artemis, Leto, Maia, Europe, Danae, and Antiope, or
that saw what he ventured to take in hand with regard to his own sister,
in having the same woman as wife and sister, would not scorn him and
pronounce him worthy of death? For not only did he commit adultery,
but he deified and raised to heaven those born of his adulteries, contriving the deification as a veil for his lawlessness: such as Dionysus,
Heracles, the Dioscuri, Hermes, Perseus, and Soteira. 2. Who, that sees
the so-called gods at irreconcileable strife among themselves at Troy
on account of the Greeks and Trojans, will fail to recognise their feebleness, in that because of their mutual jealousies they egged on even
mortals to strife? Who, that sees Ares and Aphrodite wounded by Diomed, or Hera and Aïdoneus from below the earth, whom they call a
god, wounded by Heracles, Dionysus by Perseus, Athena by Arcas,
and Hephæstus hurled down and going lame, will not recognise their
real nature, and, while refusing to call them gods, be assured (when he
hears that they are corruptible and passible) that they are nothing but
men [128] , and feeble men too, and admire those that inflicted the
wounds rather than the wounded? 3. Or who that sees the adultery of
Ares with Aphrodite, and Hephæstus contriving a snare for the two,
and the other so-called gods called by Hephæstus to view the adultery,
and coming and seeing their licentiousness, would not laugh and recognise their worthless character? Or who would not laugh at beholding
the drunken folly and misconduct of Heracles toward Omphale? For
their deeds of pleasure, and their unconscionable loves, and their divine images in gold, silver, bronze, iron, stone, and wood, we need not
seriously expose by argument, since the facts are abominable in them-

selves, and are enough taken alone to furnish proof of the deception; so that one's principal feeling is pity for those deceived about them. 4. For, hating the adulterer who tampers with a wife of their own, they are not ashamed to deify the teachers of adultery; and refraining from incest themselves they worship those who practise it; and admitting that the corrupting of children is an evil, they serve those who stand accused of it and do not blush to ascribe to those they call gods things which the laws forbid to exist even among men.

[128] This explanation of gods as deified men is known as Euhemerism, from Euhemerus, who broached the theory in the third century, b.c. (supra, 10, note 1); but there were Euhemerists in Greece before Euhemerus' (Jowett's Plato, 2. 101). The Fathers very commonly adopt the theory, for which, however, there are very slight grounds. Such cases as those of Antinous and the Emperors, as well as the legends of heroes and demigods, gave it some plausibility (see Döllinger; Gentile and Jew, vol. i. p. 344, Eng. Tr.).

§13.

The folly of image worship and its dishonour to art.

Again, in worshipping things of wood and stone, they do not see that, while they tread under foot and burn what is in no way different, they call portions of these materials gods. And what they made use of a little while ago, they carve and worship in their folly, not seeing, nor at all considering that they are worshipping, not gods, but the carver's art. 2. For so long as the stone is uncut and the wood unworked, they walk upon the one and make frequent use of the other for their own purposes, even for those which are less honourable. But when the artist has invested them with the proportions of his own skill, and impressed upon the material the form of man or woman, then, thanking the artist, they proceed to worship them as gods, having bought them from the carver at a price. Often, moreover, the image-maker, as though forgetting the work he has done himself, prays to his own productions, and calls gods what just before he was paring and chipping. 3. But it were better, if need to admire these things, to ascribe it to the art of the skilled workman, and not to honour productions in preference to their producer. For it is not the material that has adorned the art, but the art that has adorned and deified the material. Much juster were it, then, for them to worship the artist than his productions, both because his existence was prior to that of the gods produced by art, and because they have come into being in the form he pleased to give them. But as it is, setting justice aside, and dishonouring skill and art, they worship the products of skill and art, and when the man is dead that made them, they honour his works as immortal, whereas if they did not receive daily attention they would certainly in time come to a natural end. 4. Or how could one fail to pity them in this also, in that seeing, they worship them that cannot see, and hearing, pray to them that cannot hear, and born with life and reason, men as they are, call gods things which do not move at all, but have not even life, and, strangest of all, in that they serve as their masters beings whom they themselves keep under their own power? Nor imagine that this is a mere statement of mine, nor that I am maligning them; for the verification of all this meets the eyes, and whoever wishes to do so may see the like.

§14.

Image worship condemned by Scripture.

But better testimony about all this is furnished by Holy Scripture, which tells us beforehand when it says [129] , "Their idols are silver and gold, the work of men's hands. Eyes have they and will not see; a mouth have they and will not speak; ears have they and will not hear; noses have they and will not smell; hands have they and will not handle; feet have they and will not walk; they will not speak through their throat. Like unto them be they that make them." Nor have they escaped prophetic censure; for there also is their refutation, where the Spirit says [130] , "they shall be ashamed that have formed a god, and carved all of them that which is vain: and all by whom they were made are dried up: and let the deaf ones among men all assemble and stand up together, and let them be confounded and put to shame together; for the carpenter sharpened iron, and worked it with an adze, and fashioned it with an auger, and set it up with the arm of his strength: and he shall hunger and be faint, and drink no water. For the carpenter chose out wood, and set it by a rule, and fashioned it with glue, and made it as the form of a man and as the beauty of man, and set it up in his house, wood which he had cut from the grove and which the Lord planted, and the rain gave it growth that it might be for men to burn, and that he might take thereof and warm himself, and kindle, and bake bread upon it, but the residue they made into gods, and worshipped them, the half whereof they had burned in the fire. And upon the half thereof he roasted flesh and ate and was filled, and was warmed and said: It is pleasant to me, because I am warmed and have seen the fire.' But the residue thereof he worshipped, saying, Deliver me for thou art my god.' They knew not nor understood, because their eyes were dimmed that they could not see, nor perceive with their heart; nor did he consider in his heart nor know in his understanding that he had burned half thereof in the fire, and baked bread upon the coals thereof, and roasted flesh and eaten it, and made the residue thereof an abomination, and they worship it. Know that their heart is dust and they are deceived, and none can deliver his soul. Behold and will ye not say, There is a lie in my right hand?"' 2. How then can they fail to be judged godless by all, who even by the divine Scripture are accused of impiety? or how can they be anything but miserable, who are thus openly convicted of worshipping dead things instead of the truth? or what kind of hope have they? or what kind of excuse could be made for them, trusting in things without sense or movement, which they reverence in place of the true God?

[129] Ps. cxv. 5 sqq.
[130] Isa. xliv. 9 sqq. (LXX.).

§15.

The details about the gods conveyed in the representations of them by poets and artists shew that they are without life, and that they are not gods, nor even decent men and women.

For would that the artist would fashion the gods even without shape, so that they might not be open to so manifest an exposure of their lack of sense. For they might have cajoled the perception of simple folk to think the idols had senses, were it not that they possess the symbols of the senses, eyes for example and noses and ears and hands and mouth, without any gesture of actual perception and grasp of the objects of sense. But as a matter of fact they have these things and have them not, stand and stand not, sit and sit not. For they have not the real action of these things, but as their fashioner pleased, so they remain stationary, giving no sign of a god, but evidently mere inanimate objects, set there by man's art. 2. Or would that the heralds and prophets of these false gods, poets I mean and writers, had simply written that they were gods, and not also recounted their actions as an exposure of their godlessness and scandalous life. For by the mere name of godhead they might have filched away the truth, or rather have caused the mass of men to err from the truth. But as it is, by narrating the loves and immoralities of Zeus, and the corruptions of youths by the other gods, and the voluptuous jealousies of the females, and the fears and acts of cowardice and other wickednesses, they merely convict themselves of narrating not merely about no gods, but not even about respectable men, but on the contrary, of telling tales about shameful persons far removed from what is honourable.

§16

Heathen arguments in palliation of the above: and (1) the poets
are responsible for these unedifying tales.' But are the names and
existence of the gods any better authenticated? Both stand or fall
together. Either the actions must be defended or the deity of the
gods given up. And the heroes are not credited with acts inconsistent with their nature, as, on this plea, the gods are.

But perhaps, as to all this, the impious will appeal to the peculiar style of poets, saying that it is the peculiarity of poets to feign
what is not, and, for the pleasure of their hearers, to tell fictitious tales;
and that for this reason they have composed the stories about gods. But
this pretext of theirs, even more than any other, will appear to be su-
perficial from what they themselves think and profess about these
matters. 2. For if what is said in the poets is fictitious and false, even
the nomenclature of Zeus, Cronos, Hera, Ares and the rest must be
false. For perhaps, as they say, even the names are fictitious, and,
while no such being exists as Zeus, Cronos, or Ares, the poets feign
their existence to deceive their hearers. But if the poets feign the existence of unreal beings, how is it that they worship them as though they
existed? 3. Or perhaps, once again, they will say that while the names
are not fictitious, they ascribe to them fictitious actions. But even this
is equally precarious as a defence. For if they made up the actions,
doubtless also they made up the names, to which they attributed the
actions. Or if they tell the truth about the names, it follows that they
tell the truth about the actions too. In particular, they who have said in
their tales that these are gods certainly know how gods ought to act,
and would never ascribe to gods the ideas of men, any more than one
would ascribe to water the properties of fire; for fire burns, whereas
the nature of water on the contrary is cold. 4. If then the actions are
worthy of gods, they that do them must be gods; but if they are actions
of men, and of disreputable men, such as adultery and the acts men-

tioned above, they that act in such ways must be men and not gods. For their deeds must correspond to their natures, so that at once the actor may be made known by his act, and the action may be ascertainable from his nature. So that just as a man discussing about water and fire, and declaring their action, would not say that water burned and fire cooled, nor, if a man were discoursing about the sun and the earth, would he say the earth gave light, while the sun was sown with herbs and fruits, but if he were to say so would exceed the utmost height of madness, so neither would their writers, and especially the most eminent poet of all, if they really knew that Zeus and the others were gods, invest them with such actions as shew them to be not gods, but rather men, and not sober men. 5. Or if, as poets, they told falsehoods, and you are maligning them, why did they not also tell falsehoods about the courage of the heroes, and feign feebleness in the place of courage, and courage in that of feebleness? For they ought in that case, as with Zeus and Hera, so also to slanderously accuse Achilles of want of courage, and to celebrate the might of Thersites, and, while charging Odysseus with dulness, to make out Nestor a reckless person, and to narrate effeminate actions of Diomed and Hector, and manly deeds of Hecuba. For the fiction and falsehood they ascribe to the poets ought to extend to all cases. But in fact, they kept the truth for their men, while not ashamed to tell falsehoods about their so-called gods. 6. And as some of them might argue, that they are telling falsehoods about their licentious actions, but that in their praises, when they speak of Zeus as father of gods, and as the highest, and the Olympian, and as reigning in heaven, they are not inventing but speaking truthfully; this is a plea which not only myself, but anybody can refute. For the truth will be clear, in opposition to them, if we recall our previous proofs. For while their actions prove them to be men, the panegyrics upon them go beyond the nature of men. The two things then are mutually inconsistent; for neither is it the nature of heavenly beings to act in such ways, nor can any one suppose that persons so acting are gods.

<h1 style="text-align:center">§17</h1>

The truth probably is, that the scandalous tales are true, while the divine attributes ascribed to them are due to the flattery of the poets.

What inference then is left to us, save that while the panegyrics are false and flattering, the actions told of them are true? And the truth of this one can ascertain by common practice. For nobody who pronounces a panegyric upon anyone accuses his conduct at the same time, but rather, if men's actions are disgraceful, they praise them up with panegyrics, on account of the scandal they cause, so that by extravagant praise they may impose upon their hearers, and hide the misconduct of the others. 2. Just as if a man who has to pronounce a panegyric upon someone cannot find material for it in their conduct or in any personal qualities, on account of the scandal attaching to these, he praises them up in another manner, flattering them with what does not belong to them, so have their marvellous poets, put out of countenance by the scandalous actions of their so-called gods, attached to them the superhuman title, not knowing that they cannot by their superhuman fancies veil their human actions, but that they will rather succeed in shewing, by their human shortcomings, that the attributes of God do not fit them. 3. And I am disposed to think that they have recounted the passions and the actions of the gods even in spite of themselves. For since they were endeavouring to invest with what Scripture calls the incommunicable name and honour of [131] God them that are no gods but mortal men, and since this venture of theirs was great and impious, for this reason even against their will they were forced by truth to set forth the passions of these persons, so that their passions recorded in the writings concerning them might be in evidence for all posterity as a proof that they were no gods.

[131] Wisd. xiv. 21. Cf. Isa. xlii. 8, and xlviii. 11

§18

Heathen defence continued. (2) The gods are worshipped for having invented the Arts of Life.' But this is a human and natural, not a divine, achievement. And why, on this principle, are not all inventors deified?

What defence, then, what proof that these are real gods, can they offer who hold this superstition? For, by what has been said just above, our argument has demonstrated them to be men, and not respectable men. But perhaps they will turn to another argument, and proudly appeal to the things useful to life discovered by them, saying that the reason why they regard them as gods is their having been of use to mankind. For Zeus is said to have possessed the plastic art, Poseidon that of the pilot, Hephæstus the smith's, Athena that of weaving, Apollo that of music, Artemis that of hunting, Hera dressmaking, Demeter agriculture, and others other arts, as those who inform us about them have related. 2. But men ought to ascribe them and such like arts not to the gods alone but to the common nature of mankind, for by observing nature [132] men discover the arts. For even common parlance calls art an imitation of nature. If then they have been skilled in the arts they pursued, that is no reason for thinking them gods, but rather for thinking them men; for the arts were not their creation, but in them they, like others, imitated nature. 3. For men having a natural capacity for knowledge according to the definition laid down [133] concerning them, there is nothing to surprise us if by human intelligence, and by looking of themselves at their own nature and coming to know it, they have hit upon the arts. Or if they say that the discovery of the arts entitles them to be proclaimed as gods, it is high time to proclaim as gods the discoverers of the other arts on the same grounds as the former were thought worthy of such a title. For the Phoenicians invented letters, Homer epic poetry, Zeno of Elea dialectic, Corax of Syracuse rhetoric, Aristæus bee-keeping, Triptolemus the sowing of corn, Lycurgus of Sparta and Solon of Athens laws; while Palamedes discovered the arrangement of letters, and numbers, and measures and weights. And others imparted various other things useful for the life of mankind, according to the testimony of our historians. 4. If then the arts make gods, and because of them carved gods exist, it follows, on their shewing, that those who at a later date discovered the other arts must be gods. Or if they do not deem these worthy of divine honour, but recognise that they are men, it were but consistent not to give even the name of gods to Zeus, Hera, and the others, but to believe that they too have been human beings, and all the more so, inasmuch as they were not even respectable in their day; just as by the very fact of sculpturing their form in statues they shew that they are nothing else but men.

[132] phusis is here used in a double sense.

[133] By Aristotle, Top. V. ii.-iv. where man is defined as zoon epistemes dektikon: compare Metaph. I. i. All men by nature desire to know.'

§19

The inconsistency of image worship. Arguments in palliation.
(1) The divine nature must be expressed in a visible sign. (2) The
image a means of supernatural communications to men through
angels.

For what other form do they give them by sculpture but that
of men and women and of creatures lower yet and of irrational nature,
all manner of birds, beasts both tame and wild, and creeping things,
whatsoever land and sea and the whole realm of the waters produce?
For men having fallen into the unreasonableness of their passions and
pleasures, and unable to see anything beyond pleasures and lusts of the
flesh, inasmuch as they keep their mind in the midst of these irrational
things, they imagined the divine principle to be in irrational things, and
carved a number of gods to match the variety of their passions. 2. For
there are with them images of beasts and creeping things and birds, as
the interpreter of the divine and true religion says, "They became vain
in their reasonings, and their senseless heart was darkened. Professing
themselves to be wise, they became fools, and changed the glory of the
incorruptible God for the likeness of an image of corruptible man, and
of birds and four-footed beasts and creeping things, wherefore God
gave them up unto vile passions." For having previously infected their
soul, as I said above, with the irrationalities of pleasures, they then
came down to this making of gods; and, once fallen, thenceforward as
though abandoned in their rejection of God, thus they wallow [134] in
them, and portray God, the Father of the Word, in irrational shapes. 3.
As to which those who pass for philosophers and men of knowledge
[135] among the Greeks, while driven to admit that their visible gods are
the forms and figures of men and of irrational objects, say in defence
that they have such things to the end that by their means the deity may
answer them and be made manifest; because otherwise they could not
know the invisible God, save by such statues and rites. 4. While those

[136] who profess to give still deeper and more philosophical reasons than these say, that the reason of idols being prepared and fashioned is for the invocation and manifestation of divine angels and powers, that appearing by these means they may teach men concerning the knowledge of God; and that they serve as letters for men, by referring to which they may learn to apprehend God, from the manifestation of the divine angels effected by their means. Such then is their mythology,-- for far be it from us to call it a theology. But if one examine the argument with care, he will find that the opinion of these persons also, not less than that of those previously spoken of, is false.

[134] Cf. Orat. iii. 16.

[135] This may refer to Maximus of Tyre (Saussaye, §11), or to the lost-treatise of the divine Iamblichus' Peri agalmaton, which was considered worth answering by Christian writers as late as the seventh century (Philoponus in Phot. Bibl. Cod. 215).

[136] This is in effect the defence of the Scriptor de Mysteriis' (possibly Iamblichus, see Bernays 2 Abhandlungen' 1880, p. 37): material means of worship are a means of access directly to the lower (or quasi-material) gods, and so indirectly to the higher. Few men can reach the latter without the aid of their manifestation in the lower; parestin a& 204;los tois enulois ta a& 203;la (v. 23, cf. 14).

§20

But where does this supposed virtue of the image reside? in the material, or in the form, or in the maker's skill? Untenability of all these views.

For one might reply to them, bringing the case before the tribunal of truth, How does God make answer or become known by such objects? Is it due to the matter of which they consist, or to the form which they possess? For if it be due to the matter, what need is there of the form, instead of God manifesting Himself through all matter without exception before these things were fashioned? And in vain have they built their temples to shut in a single stone, or stock, or piece of gold, when all the world is full of these substances. 2. But if the superadded form be the cause of the divine manifestation, what is the need of the material, gold and the rest, instead of God manifesting Himself by the actual natural animals of which the images are the figures? For the opinion held about God would on the same principle have been a nobler one, were He to manifest Himself by means of living animals, whether rational or irrational, instead of being looked for in things without life or motion. 3. Wherein they commit the most signal impiety against themselves. For while they abominate and turn from the real animals, beasts, birds, and creeping things, either because of their ferocity or because of their dirtiness, yet they carve their forms in stone, wood, or gold, and make them gods. But it would be better for them to worship the living things themselves, rather than to worship their figures in stone. 4. But perhaps neither is the case, nor is either the material or the form the cause of the divine presence, but it is only skilful art that summons the deity, inasmuch as it is an imitation of nature. But if the deity communicates with the inmates on account of the art, what need, once more, of the material, since the art resides in the men? For if God manifests Himself solely because of the art, and if for this reason the images are worshipped as gods, it would be right to worship and serve the men who are masters of the art, inasmuch as they are rational also, and have the skill in themselves.

<h1 style="text-align:center">§21</h1>

The idea of communications through angels involves yet wilder inconsistency, nor does it, even if true, justify the worship of the image.

But as to their second and as they say profounder defence, one might reasonably add as follows. If these things are made by you, ye Greeks, not for the sake of a self-manifestation of God Himself, but for the sake of a presence there of angels, why do you rank the images by which ye invoke the powers as superior and above the powers invoked? For ye carve the figures for the sake of the apprehension of God, as ye say, but invest the actual images with the honour and title of God, thus placing yourselves in a profane position. 2. For while confessing that the power of God transcends the littleness of the images, and for that reason not venturing to invoke God through them, but only the lesser powers, ye yourselves leap over these latter, and have bestowed on stocks and stones the title of Him, whose presence ye feared, and call them gods instead of stones and men's workmanship, and worship them. For even supposing them to serve you, as ye falsely say, as letters for the contemplation of God, it is not right to give the signs greater honour than that which they signify. For neither if a man were to write the emperor's name would it be without risk to give to the writing more honour than to the emperor; on the contrary, such a man incurs the penalty of death; while the writing is fashioned by the skill of the writer. 3. So also yourselves, had ye your reasoning power in full strength, would not reduce to matter so great a revelation of the Godhead: but neither would ye have given to the image greater honour than to the man that carved it. For if there be any truth in the plea that, as letters, they indicate the manifestation of God, and are therefore, as indications of God, worthy to be deified, yet far more would it be right to deify the artist who carved and engraved them, as being far more powerful and divine than they, inasmuch as they were cut and fashioned according to his will. If then the letters are worthy of admiration, much more does the writer exceed them in wonder, by reason of his art and the skill of his mind. If then it be not fitting to think that they are gods for this reason, one must again interrogate them about the madness concerning the idols, demanding from them the justification for their being in such a form.

§22

The image cannot represent the true form of God, else God
would be corruptible.

For if the reason of their being thus fashioned is, that the Deity is of human form, why do they invest it also with the forms of irrational creatures? Or if the form of it is that of the latter, why do they embody it also in the images of rational creatures? Or if it be both at once, and they conceive God to be of the two combined, namely, that He has the forms both of rational and of irrational, why do they separate what is joined together, and separate the images of brutes and of men, instead of always carving it of both kinds, such as are the fictions in the myths, Scylla, Charybdis, the Hippocentaur, and the dog-headed Anubis of the Egyptians? For they ought either to represent them solely of two natures in this way, or, if they have a single form, not to falsely represent them in the other as well. 2. And again, if their forms are male, why do they also invest them with female shapes? Or if they are of the latter, why do they also falsify their forms as though they were males? Or if again they are a mixture of both, they ought not to be divided, but both ought to be combined, and follow the type of the so-called hermaphrodites, so that their superstition should furnish beholders with a spectacle not only of impiety and calumny, but of ridicule as well. 2. And generally, if they conceive the Deity to be corporeal, so that they contrive for it and represent belly and hands and feet, and neck also, and breasts and the other organs that go to make man, see to what impiety and godlessness their mind has come down, to have such ideas of the Deity. For it follows that it must be capable of all other bodily casualties as well, of being cut and divided, and even of perishing altogether. But these and like things are not properties of God, but rather of earthly bodies. 3. For while God is incorporeal and incorruptible, and immortal, needing nothing for any purpose, these are both corruptible, and are shapes of bodies, and need bodily ministrations, as we said before [137] . For often we see images which have grown old renewed, and those which time, or rain, or some or other of the animals of the earth have spoiled, restored. In which connexion one must condemn their folly, in that they proclaim as gods things of which they themselves are the makers, and themselves ask salvation of objects which they themselves adorn with their arts to preserve them from corruption, and beg that their own wants may be supplied by beings which they well know need attention from themselves, and are not ashamed to call lords of heaven and all the earth creatures whom they shut up in small chambers.

[137] Supra xiii. 3.

§23

The variety of idolatrous cults proves that they are false.

But not only from these considerations may one appreciate their godlessness, but also from their discordant opinions about the idols themselves. For if they be gods according to their assertion and their speculations, to which of them is one to give allegiance, and which of them is one to judge to be the higher, so as either to worship God with confidence, or as they say to recognise the Deity by them without ambiguity? For not the same beings are called gods among all; on the contrary, for every nation almost there is a separate god imagined. And there are cases of a single district and a single town being at internal discord about the superstition of their idols. 2. The Phoenicians, for example, do not know those who are called gods among the Egyptians, nor do the Egyptians worship the same idols as the Phoenicians have. And while the Scythians reject the gods of the Persians, the Persians reject those of the Syrians. But the Pelasgians also repudiate the gods in Thrace, while the Thracians know not those of Thebes. The Indians moreover differ from the Arabs, the Arabs from the Ethiopians, and the Ethiopians from the Arabs in their idols. And the Syrians worship not the idols of the Cilicians, while the Cappadocian nation call gods beings different from these. And while the Bithynians have adopted others, the Armenians have imagined others again. And what need is there for me to multiply examples? The men on the continent worship other gods than the islanders, while these latter serve other gods than those of the main lands. 3. And, in general, every city and village, not knowing the gods of its neighbours, prefers its own, and deems that these alone are gods. For concerning the abominations in Egypt there is no need even to speak, as they are before the eyes of all: how the cities have religions which are opposite and incompatible, and neighbours always make a point of worshipping the opposite of those next to them [138] : so much so that the crocodile, prayed to by some, is held in abomination by their neighbours, while the lion, worshipped as a god by others, their neighbours, so far from worshipping, slay, if they find it, as a wild beast; and the fish, consecrated by some people, is used as food in another place. And thus arise fights and riots and frequent occasions of bloodshed, and every indulgence of the passions among them. 4. And strange to say, according to the statement of historians, the very Pelasgians, who learned from the Egyptians the names of the gods, do not know the gods of Egypt, but worship others instead. And, speaking generally, all the nations that are infatuated with idols have different opinions and religions, and consistency is not to be met with in any one case. Nor is this surprising. 5. For having fallen from the contemplation of the one God, they have come down to many and diverse objects; and having turned from the Word of the Father, Christ the Saviour of all, they naturally have their understanding wandering in many directions. And just as men who have turned from the sun and are come into dark places go round by many pathless ways, and see not those who are present, while they imagine those to be there who are not, and seeing see not; so they that have turned from God and whose soul is darkened, have their mind in a roving state, and like men who are drunk and cannot see, imagine what is not true.

[138] Hdt. ii. 69; cf. Juv. Sat. xv. 36, numina vicinorum Odit uterque locus.' This is one of the few places where Athanasius has any Egyptian local colour' (cf. supra 9 and 10). M. Fialon is certainly too imaginative (p. 86 contradicted p. 283), when he sees in the contra Gentes an appreciation of the higher religious principles which the modern science (toute Francaise') of Egyptology has enabled us to read behind the grotesque features of popular Egyptian polytheism.

§24

The so-called gods of one place are used as victims in another.

This, then, is no slight proof of their real godlessness. For, the gods for every city and country being many and various, and the one destroying the god of the other, the whole of them are destroyed by all. For those who are considered gods by some are offered as sacrifices and drink-offerings to the so-called gods of others, and the victims of some are conversely the gods of others. So the Egyptians serve the ox, and Apis, a calf, and others sacrifice these animals to Zeus. For even if they do not sacrifice the very animals the others have consecrated, yet by sacrificing their fellows they seem to offer the same. The Libyans have for god a sheep which they call Ammon, and in other nations this animal is slain as a victim to many gods. 2. The Indians worship Dionysus, using the name as a symbol for wine, and others pour out wine as an offering to the other gods. Others honour rivers and springs, and above all the Egyptians pay especial honour to water, calling them gods. And yet others, and even the Egyptians who worship the waters, use them to wash off the dirt from others and from themselves, and ignominiously throw away what is used. While nearly the whole of the Egyptian system of idols consists of what are victims to the gods of other nations, so that they are scorned even by those others for deifying what are not gods, but, both with others and even among themselves, propitiatory offerings and victims.

§25

Human sacrifice. Its absurdity. Its prevalence. Its calamitous results.

But some have been led by this time to such a pitch of irreligion and folly as to slay and to offer in sacrifice to their false gods even actual men, whose figures and forms the gods are. Nor do they see, wretched men, that the victims they are slaying are the patterns of the gods they make and worship, and to whom they are offering the men. For they are offering, one may say, equals to equals, or rather, the higher to the lower; for they are offering living creatures to dead, and rational beings to things without motion. 2. For the Scythians who are called Taurians offer in sacrifice to their Virgin, as they call her, survivors from wrecks, and such Greeks as they catch, going thus far in impiety against men of their own race, and thus exposing the savagery of their gods, in that those whom Providence has rescued from danger and from the sea, they slay, almost fighting against Providence; because they frustrate the kindness of Providence by their own brutal character. But others, when they are returned victorious from war, thereupon dividing their prisoners into hundreds, and taking a man from each, sacrifice to Ares the man they have picked out from each hundred. 3. Nor is it only Scythians who commit these abominations on account of the ferocity natural to them as barbarians: on the contrary, this deed is a special result of the wickedness connected with idols and false gods. For the Egyptians used formerly to offer victims of this kind to Hera, and the Phoenicians and Cretans used to propitiate Cronos in their sacrifices of children. And even the ancient Romans used to worship Jupiter Latiarius, as he was called, with human sacrifices, and some in one way, some in another, but all [139] without exception committed and incurred the pollution: they incurred it by the mere perpetration of the murderous deeds, while they polluted their own temples by filling them with the smoke of such sacrifices. 4. This then was the ready source of numerous evils to mankind. For seeing that their false gods were pleased with these things, they forthwith imitated their gods with like misdoings, thinking that the imitation of superior beings, as they considered them, was a credit to themselves. Hence mankind was thinned by murders of grown men and children, and by licence of all kinds. For nearly every city is full of licentiousness of all kinds, the result of the savage character of its gods; nor is there one of sober life in the idols' temples [140] save only he whose licentiousness is witnessed to by them all [141] .

[139] On human sacrifice see Saussaye, §17, and Robertson Smith, Religion of the Semites, pp. 343 sqq., especially p. 347, note 1, for references to examples near the time of this treatise.

[140] Reading eidoleiois conj. Marr.

[141] i.e. among the licentious worshippers the lifeless image is the only one free from vice, although the worshippers credit him with divine attributes, and therefore, according to their superstition, with a licentious life.

§26

The moral corruptions of Paganism all admittedly originated
with the gods.

Women, for example, used to sit out in old days in the temples of Phoenicia, consecrating to the gods there the hire of their bodies, thinking they propitiated their goddess by fornication, and that they would procure her favour by this. While men, denying their nature, and no longer wishing to be males, put on the guise of women, under the idea that they are thus gratifying and honouring the Mother of their so-called gods. But all live along with the basest, and vie with the worst among themselves, and as Paul said, the holy minister of Christ [142] : "For their women changed the natural use into that which is against nature: and likewise also the men, leaving the natural use of the woman, burned in their lust one toward another, men with men working unseemliness." 2. But acting in this and in like ways, they admit and prove that the life of their so-called gods was of the same kind. For from Zeus they have learned corruption of youth and adultery, from Aphrodite fornication, from Rhea licentiousness, from Ares murders, and from other gods other like things, which the laws punish and from which every sober man turns away. Does it then remain fit to consider them gods who do such things, instead of reckoning them, for the licentiousness of their ways, more irrational than the brutes? Is it fit to consider their worshippers human beings, instead of pitying them as more irrational than the brutes, and more soul-less than inanimate things? For had they considered the intellectual part of their soul they would not have plunged headlong into these things, nor have denied the true God, the Father of Christ.

[142] Rom. i. 26.

§27

The refutation of popular Paganism being taken as conclusive,
we come to the higher form of nature-worship. How Nature witnesses to God by the mutual dependence of all her parts, which
forbid us to think of any one of them as the supreme God. This
shewn at length.

But perhaps those who have advanced beyond these things,
and who stand in awe of Creation, being put to shame by these expo-
sures of abominations, will join in repudiating what is readily
condemned and refuted on all hands, but will think that they have a
well-grounded and unanswerable opinion, namely, the worship of the
universe and of the parts of the universe. 2. For they will boast that
they worship and serve, not mere stocks and stones and forms of men
and irrational birds and creeping things and beasts, but the sun and
moon and all the heavenly universe, and the earth again, and the entire
realm of water: and they will say that none can shew that these at any
rate are not of divine nature, since it is evident to all, that they lack
neither life nor reason, but transcend even the nature of mankind, inasmuch as the one inhabit the heavens, the other the earth. 3. It is
worth while then to look into and examine these points also; for here,
too, our argument will find that its proof against them holds true. But
before we look, or begin our demonstration, it suffices that Creation
almost raises its voice against them, and points to God as its Maker
and Artificer, Who reigns over Creation and over all things, even the
Father of our Lord Jesus Christ; Whom the would-be philosophers turn
from to worship and deify the Creation which proceeded from Him,
which yet itself worships and confesses the Lord Whom they deny on
its account. 4. For if men are thus awestruck at the parts of Creation
and think that they are gods, they might well be rebuked by the mutual
dependence of those parts; which moreover makes known, and witnesses to, the Father of the Word, Who is the Lord and Maker of these
parts also, by the unbroken law of their obedience to Him, as the divine law also says: "The heavens declare the glory of God, and the
firmament sheweth His handiwork [143] ." 5. But the proof of all this is
not obscure, but is clear enough in all conscience to those the eyes of

whose understanding are not wholly disabled. For if a man take the parts of Creation separately, and consider each by itself,--as for example the sun by itself alone, and the moon apart, and again earth and air, and heat and cold, and the essence of wet and of dry, separating them from their mutual conjunction,--he will certainly find that not one is sufficient for itself but all are in need of one another's assistance, and subsist by their mutual help. For the Sun is carried round along with, and is contained in, the whole heaven, and can never go beyond his own orbit, while the moon and other stars testify to the assistance given them by the Sun: while the earth again evidently does not yield her crops without rains, which in their turn would not descend to earth without the assistance of the clouds; but not even would the clouds ever appear of themselves and subsist, without the air. And the air is warmed by the upper air, but illuminated and made bright by the sun, not by itself. 6. And wells, again, and rivers will never exist without the earth; but the earth is not supported upon itself, but is set upon the realm of the waters, while this again is kept in its place, being bound fast at the centre of the universe. And the sea, and the great ocean that flows outside round the whole earth, is moved and borne by winds wherever the force of the winds dashes it. And the winds in their turn originate, not in themselves, but according to those who have written on the subject, in the air, from the burning heat and high temperature of the upper as compared with the lower air, and blow everywhere through the latter. 7. For as to the four elements of which the nature of bodies is composed, heat, that is, and cold, wet and dry, who is so perverted in his understanding as not to know that these things exist indeed in combination, but if separated and taken alone they tend to destroy even one another according to the prevailing power of the more abundant element? For heat is destroyed by cold if it be present in greater quantity, and cold again is put away by the power of heat, and what is dry, again, is moistened by wet, and the latter dried by the former.

[143] Ps. xix. 1.

§28

But neither can the cosmic organism be God. For that would make God consist of dissimilar parts, and subject Him to possible dissolution.

How then can these things be gods, seeing that they need one another's assistance? Or how is it proper to ask anything of them when they too ask help for themselves one from another? For if it is an admitted truth about God that He stands in need of nothing, but is self-sufficient and self-contained, and that in Him all things have their being, and that He ministers to all rather than they to Him, how is it right to proclaim as gods the sun and moon and other parts of creation, which are of no such kind, but which even stand in need of one another's help? 2. But, perhaps, if divided and taken by themselves, our opponents themselves will admit that they are dependent, the demonstration being an ocular one. But they will combine all together, as constituting a single body, and will say that the whole is God. For the whole once put together, they will no longer need external help, but the whole will be sufficient for itself and independent in all respects; so at least the would-be philosophers will tell us, only to be refuted here once more. 3. Now this argument, not one whit less than those previously dealt with, will demonstrate their impiety coupled with great ignorance. For if the combination of the parts makes up the whole, and the whole is combined out of the parts, then the whole consists of the parts, and each of them is a portion of the whole. But this is very far removed from the conception of God. For God is a whole and not a number of parts, and does not consist of diverse elements, but is Himself the Maker of the system of the universe. For see what impiety they utter against the Deity when they say this. For if He consists of parts, certainly it will follow that He is unlike Himself, and made up of unlike parts. For if He is sun, He is not moon, and if He is moon, He is not earth, and if He is earth, He cannot be sea: and so on, taking the parts one by one, one may discover the absurdity of this theory of theirs. 4. But the following point, drawn from the observation of our human body, is enough to refute them. For just as the eye is not the sense of hearing, nor is the latter a hand: nor is the belly the breast, nor again is the neck a foot, but each of these has its own function, and a single body is composed of these distinct parts,--having its parts combined for use, but destined to be divided in course of time when nature, that brought them together, shall divide them at the will of God, Who so ordered it;--thus (but may He that is above pardon the argument [144]), if they combine the parts of creation into one body and proclaim it God, it follows, firstly, that He is unlike Himself, as shewn above; secondly, that He is destined to be divided again, in accordance with the natural tendency of the parts to separation.

[144] Cf. Orat. i. 25, note 2.

§29

The balance of powers in Nature shews that it is not God, either collectively, or in parts.

And in yet another way one may refute their godlessness by the light of truth. For if God is incorporeal and invisible and intangible by nature, how do they imagine God to be a body, and worship with divine honour things which we both see with our eyes and touch with our hands? 2. And again, if what is said of God hold true, namely, that He is almighty, and that while nothing has power over Him, He has power and rule over all, how can they who deify creation fail to see that it does not satisfy this definition of God? For when the sun is under the earth, the earth's shadow makes his light invisible, while by day the sun hides the moon by the brilliancy of his light. And hail ofttimes injures the fruits of the earth, while fire is put out if an overflow of water take place. And spring makes winter give place, while summer will not suffer spring to outstay its proper limits, and it in its turn is forbidden by autumn to outstep its own season. 3. If then they were gods, they ought not to be defeated and obscured by one another, but always to co-exist, and to discharge their respective functions simultaneously. Both by night and by day the sun and the moon and the rest of the band of stars ought to shine equally together, and give their light to all, so that all things might be illumined by them. Spring and summer and autumn and winter ought to go on without alteration, and together. The sea ought to mingle with the springs, and furnish their drink to man in common. Calms and windy blasts ought to take place at the same time. Fire and water together ought to furnish the same service to man. For no one would take any hurt from them, if they are gods, as our opponents say, and do nothing for hurt, but rather all things for good. 4. But if none of these things are possible, because of their mutual incompatibility, how does it remain possible to give to these things, mutually incompatible and at strife, and unable to combine, the name of gods, or to worship them with the honours due to God? How could things naturally discordant give peace to others for their prayers, and become to them authors of concord? It is not then likely that the sun or the moon, or any other part of creation, still less statues in stone, gold, or other material, or the Zeus, Apollo, and the rest, who are the subject of the poet's fables, are true gods: this our argument has shewn. But some of these are parts of creation, others have no life, others have been mere mortal men. Therefore their worship and deification is no part of religion, but the bringing in of godlessness and of all impiety, and a sign of a wide departure from the knowledge of the one true God, namely the Father of Christ. 5. Since then this is thus proved, and the idolatry of the Greeks is shewn to be full of all ungodliness, and that its introduction has been not for the good, but for the ruin, of human life;--come now, as our argument promised at the outset, let us, after having confuted error, travel the way of truth, and behold the Leader and Artificer of the Universe, the Word of the Father, in order that through Him we may apprehend the Father, and that the Greeks may know how far they have separated themselves from the truth.

§30

The soul of man, being intellectual, can know God of itself, if it be true to its own nature.

The tenets we have been speaking of have been proved to be nothing more than a false guide for life; but the way of truth will aim at reaching the real and true God. But for its knowledge and accurate comprehension, there is need of none other save of ourselves. Neither as God Himself is above all, is the road to Him afar off or outside ourselves, but it is in us and it is possible to find it from ourselves, in the first instance, as Moses also taught, when he said [145] : "The word" of faith "is within thy heart." Which very thing the Saviour declared and confirmed, when He said: "The kingdom of God is within you [146] ." 2. For having in ourselves faith, and the kingdom of God, we shall be able quickly to see and perceive the King of the Universe, the saving Word of the Father. And let not the Greeks, who worship idols, make excuses, nor let any one else simply deceive himself, professing to have no such road and therefore finding a pretext for his godlessness. 3. For we all have set foot upon it, and have it, even if not all are willing to travel by it, but rather to swerve from it and go wrong, because of the pleasures of life which attract them from without. And if one were to ask, what road is this? I say that it is the soul of each one of us, and the intelligence which resides there. For by it alone can God be contemplated and perceived. 4. Unless, as they have denied God, the impious men will repudiate having a soul; which indeed is more plausible than the rest of what they say, for it is unlike men possessed of an intellect to deny God, its Maker and Artificer. It is necessary then, for the sake of the simple, to shew briefly that each one of mankind has a soul, and that soul rational; especially as certain of the sectaries deny this also, thinking that man is nothing more than the visible form of the body. This point once proved, they will be furnished in their own persons with a clearer proof against the idols.

[145] Deut. xxx. 14.
[146] Luc. xvii. 12.

§31

Proof of the existence of the rational soul. (1) Difference of man
from the brutes. (2) Man's power of objective thought. Thought
is to sense as the musician to his instrument. The phenomena of
dreams bear this out.

Firstly, then, the rational nature of the soul is strongly confirmed by its difference from irrational creatures. For this is why
common use gives them that name, because, namely, the race of mankind is rational. 2. Secondly, it is no ordinary proof, that man alone
thinks of things external to himself, and reasons about things not actually present, and exercises reflection, and chooses by judgment the
better of alternative reasonings. For the irrational animals see only
what is present, and are impelled solely by what meets their eye, even
if the consequences to them are injurious, while man is not impelled
toward what he sees merely, but judges by thought what he sees with
his eyes. Often for example his impulses are mastered by reasoning;
and his reasoning is subject to after-reflection. And every one, if he be
a friend of truth, perceives that the intelligence of mankind is distinct
from the bodily senses. 3. Hence, because it is distinct, it acts as judge
of the senses, and while they apprehend their objects, the intelligence
distinguishes, recollects, and shews them what is best. For the sole
function of the eye is to see, of the ears to hear, of the mouth to taste,
of the nostrils to apprehend smells, and of the hands to touch. But what
one ought to see and hear, what one ought to touch, taste and smell, is
a question beyond the senses, and belonging to the soul and to the intelligence which resides in it. Why, the hand is able to take hold of a
sword-blade, and the mouth to taste poison, but neither knows that
these are injurious, unless the intellect decide. 4. And the case, to look
at it by aid of a simile, is like that of a well-fashioned lyre in the hands
of a skilled musician. For as the strings of the lyre have each its proper
note, high, low, or intermediate, sharp or otherwise, yet their scale is

indistinguishable and their time not to be recognized, without the artist. For then only is the scale manifest and the time right, when he that is holding the lyre strikes the strings and touches each in tune. In like manner, the senses being disposed in the body like a lyre, when the skilled intelligence presides over them, then too the soul distinguishes and knows what it is doing and how it is acting. 5. But this alone is peculiar to mankind, and this is what is rational in the soul of mankind, by means of which it differs from the brutes, and shews that it is truly distinct from what is to be seen in the body. Often, for example, when the body is lying on the earth, man imagines and contemplates what is in the heavens. Often when the body is quiet [147] , and at rest and asleep, man moves inwardly, and beholds what is outside himself, travelling to other countries, walking about, meeting his acquaintances, and often by these means divining and forecasting the actions of the day. But to what can this be due save to the rational soul, in which man thinks of and perceives things beyond himself?

[147] Cf. Vit. Ant. 34.

§32

(3) The body cannot originate such phenomena; and in fact the action of the rational soul is seen in its over-ruling the instincts of the bodily organs.

We add a further point to complete our demonstration for the benefit of those [148] who shamelessly take refuge in denial of reason. How is it, that whereas the body is mortal by nature, man reasons on the things of immortality, and often, where virtue demands it, courts death? Or how, since the body lasts but for a time, does man imagine of things eternal, so as to despise what lies before him, and desire what is beyond? The body could not have spontaneously such thoughts about itself, nor could it think upon what is external to itself. For it is mortal and lasts but for a time. And it follows that that which thinks what is opposed to the body and against its nature must be distinct in kind. What then can this be, save a rational and immortal soul? For it introduces the echo of higher things, not outside, but within the body, as the musician does in his lyre. 2. Or how again, the eye being naturally constituted to see and the ear to hear, do they turn from some objects and choose others? For who is it that turns away the eye from seeing? Or who shuts off the ear from hearing, its natural function? Or who often hinders the palate, to which it is natural to taste things, from its natural impulse? Or who withholds the hand from its natural activity of touching something, or turns aside the sense of smell from its normal exercise [149] ? Who is it that thus acts against the natural instincts of the body? Or how does the body, turned from its natural course, turn to the counsels of another and suffer itself to be guided at the beck of that other? Why, these things prove simply this, that the rational soul presides over the body. 3. For the body is not even constituted to drive itself, but it is carried at the will of another, just as a horse does not yoke himself, but is driven by his master. Hence laws for human beings to practise what is good and to abstain from evil-doing, while to the brutes evil remains unthought of and undiscerned, because they lie outside rationality and the process of understanding. I think then that the existence of a rational soul in man is proved by what we have said.

[148] Supra xxx.
[149] Compare the somewhat analogous argument in Butler, Serm. ii.

<h1 style="text-align:center">§33</h1>

The soul immortal. Proved by (1) its being distinct from the body, (2) its being the source of motion, (3) its power to go beyond the body in imagination and thought.

But that the soul is made immortal is a further point in the Church's teaching which you must know, to show how the idols are to be overthrown. But we shall more directly arrive at a knowledge of this from what we know of the body, and from the difference between the body and the soul. For if our argument has proved it to be distinct from the body, while the body is by nature mortal, it follows that the soul is immortal, because it is not like the body. 2. And again, if as we have shewn, the soul moves the body and is not moved by other things, it follows that the movement of the soul is spontaneous, and that this spontaneous movement goes on after the body is laid aside in the earth. If then the soul were moved by the body, it would follow that the severance of its motor would involve its death. But if the soul moves the body also, it follows all the more that it moves itself. But if moved by itself [150] , it follows that it outlives the body. 3. For the movement of the soul is the same thing as its life, just as, of course, we call the body alive when it moves, and say that its death takes place when it ceases moving. But this can be made clearer once for all from the action of the soul in the body. For if even when united and coupled with the body it is not shut in or commensurate with the small dimensions of the body, but often [151] , when the body lies in bed, not moving, but in death-like sleep, the soul keeps awake by virtue of its own power, and transcends the natural power of the body, and as though travelling away from the body while remaining in it, imagines and beholds things above the earth, and often even holds converse with the saints and angels who are above earthly and bodily existence, and approaches them in the confidence of the purity of its intelligence; shall it not all the more, when separated from the body at the time appointed by God Who coupled them together, have its knowledge of immortality more clear? For if even when coupled with the body it lived a life outside the body, much more shall its life continue after the death of the body, and live without ceasing by reason of God Who made it thus by His own Word, our Lord Jesus Christ. 4. For this is the reason why the soul thinks of and bears in mind things immortal and eternal, namely, because it is itself immortal. And just as, the body being mortal, its senses also have mortal things as their objects, so, since the soul contemplates and beholds immortal things, it follows that it is immortal and lives for ever. For ideas and thoughts about immortality never desert the soul, but abide in it, and are as it were the fuel in it which ensures its immortality. This then is why the soul has the capacity for beholding God, and is its own way thereto, receiving not from without but from herself the knowledge and apprehension of the Word of God.

[150] Cf. Plato Phædr. 245 C-E., Legg. 896, A, B. The former passage is more likely to be referred to here as it is, like the text, an argument for immortality. Athan. has also referred to Phædrus above, §5. (Against Gwatkin, Studies, p. 101.)
[151] Cp. xxxi. 5, and ref.

§34

The soul, then, if only it get rid of the stains of sin is able to know God directly, its own rational nature imaging back the Word of God, after whose image it was created. But even if it cannot pierce the cloud which sin draws over its vision, it is confronted by the witness of creation to God.

We repeat then what we said before, that just as men denied God, and worship things without soul, so also in thinking they have not a rational soul, they receive at once the punishment of their folly, namely, to be reckoned among irrational creatures: and so, since as though from lack of a soul of their own they superstitiously worship soulless gods, they are worthy of pity and guidance. 2. But if they claim to have a soul, and pride themselves on the rational principle, and that rightly, why do they, as though they had no soul, venture to go against reason, and think not as they ought, but make themselves out higher even than the Deity? For having a soul that is immortal and invisible to them, they make a likeness of God in things visible and mortal. Or why, in like manner as they have departed from God, do they not betake themselves to Him again? For they are able, as they turned away their understanding from God, and feigned as gods things that were not, in like manner to ascend with the intelligence of their soul, and turn back to God again. 3. But turn back they can, if they lay aside the filth of all lust which they have put on, and wash it away persistently, until they have got rid of all the foreign matter that has affected their soul, and can shew it in its simplicity as it was made, that so they may be able by it to behold the Word of the Father after Whose likeness they were originally made. For the soul is made after the image and likeness of God, as divine Scripture also shews, when it says in the person of God [152] : "Let us make man after our Image and likeness." Whence also when it gets rid of all the filth of sin which covers it and retains only the likeness of the Image in its purity, then surely this latter being thoroughly brightened, the soul beholds as in a mirror the Image of the Father, even the Word, and by His means reaches the idea of the Father, Whose Image the Saviour is. 4. Or, if the soul's own teaching is insufficient, by reason of the external things which cloud its intelligence, and prevent its seeing what is higher, yet it is further possible to attain to the knowledge of God from the things which are seen, since Creation, as though in written characters, declares in a loud voice, by its order and harmony, its own Lord and Creator.

[152] Gen. i. 26.

§35

Creation a revelation of God; especially in the order and harmony pervading the whole.

For God, being good and loving to mankind, and caring for
the souls made by Him,--since He is by nature invisible and incompre-
hensible, having His being beyond all created existence [153] , for which
reason the race of mankind was likely to miss the way to the knowledge of Him, since they are made out of nothing while He is unmade,--
for this cause God by His own Word gave the Universe the Order it
has, in order that since He is by nature invisible, men might be enabled
to know Him at any rate by His works [154] . For often the artist even
when not seen is known by his works. 2. And as they tell of Phidias
the Sculptor that his works of art by their symmetry and by the proportion of their parts betray Phidias to those who see them although he is
not there, so by the order of the Universe one ought to perceive God its
maker and artificer, even though He be not seen with the bodily eyes.
For God did not take His stand upon His invisible nature (let none
plead that as an excuse) and leave Himself utterly unknown to men;
but as I said above, He so ordered Creation that although He is by nature invisible He may yet be known by His works. 3. And I say this not
on my own authority, but on the strength of what I learned from men
who have spoken of God, among them Paul, who thus writes to the
Romans [155] : "for the invisible things of Him since the creation of the
world are clearly seen, being understood by the things that are made;"
while to the Lycaonians he speaks out and says [156] : "We also are men
of like passions with you, and bring you good tidings, to turn from
these vain things unto a Living God, Who made the heaven and the
earth and the sea, and all that in them is, Who in the generations gone
by suffered all nations to walk in their own ways. And yet He left not
Himself without witness, in that He did good, and gave you [157] from
heaven rains and fruitful seasons, filling your hearts with food and

gladness." 4. For who that sees the circle of heaven and the course of the sun and the moon, and the positions and movements of the other stars, as they take place in opposite and different directions, while yet in their difference all with one accord observe a consistent order, can resist the conclusion that these are not ordered by themselves, but have a maker distinct from themselves who orders them? or who that sees the sun rising by day and the moon shining by night, and waning and waxing without variation exactly according to the same number of days, and some of the stars running their courses and with orbits various and manifold, while others move [158] without wandering, can fail to perceive that they certainly have a creator to guide them?

[153] Cf. below, 40. 2.
[154] Cf. Orat. ii. 32.
[155] Rom. i. 20.
[156] Acts xiv. 15.
[157] humin and humon below are read by several mss., and are probably correct as in the original passage.
[158] The fixed' stars as distinct from the planets. For the argument, cf. Plato, Legg. 966 E.

§36

This the more striking, if we consider the opposing forces out of which this order is produced.

Who that sees things of opposite nature combined, and in concordant harmony, as for example fire mingled with cold, and dry with wet, and that not in mutual conflict, but making up a single body, as it were homogeneous, can resist the inference that there is One external to these things that has united them? Who that sees winter giving place to spring and spring to summer and summer to autumn, and that these things contrary by nature (for the one chills, the other burns, the one nourishes, the other destroys), yet all make up a balanced result beneficial to mankind,--can fail to perceive that there is One higher than they, Who balances and guides them all, even if he see Him not? 2. Who that sees the clouds supported in air, and the weight of the waters bound up in the clouds, can but perceive Him that binds them up and has ordered these things so? Or who that sees the earth, heaviest of all things by nature, fixed upon the waters, and remaining unmoved upon what is by nature mobile, will fail to understand that there is One that has made and ordered it, even God? Who that sees the earth bringing forth fruits in due season, and the rains from heaven, and the flow of rivers, and springing up of wells, and the birth of animals from unlike parents, and that these things take place not at all times but at determinate seasons,--and in general, among things mutually unlike and contrary, the balanced and uniform order to which they conform,--can resist the inference that there is one Power which orders and administers them, ordaining things well as it thinks fit? 4. For left to themselves they could not subsist or ever be able to appear, on account of their mutual contrariety of nature. For water is by nature heavy, and tends to flow downwards, while the clouds are light and belong to the class of things which tend to soar and mount upwards. And yet we see water, heavy as it is, borne aloft in the clouds. And again, earth is very heavy, while water on the other hand is relatively light; and yet the heavier is supported upon the lighter, and the earth does not sink, but remains immoveable. And male and female are not the same, while yet they unite in one, and the result is the generation from both of an animal like them. And to cut the matter short, cold is opposite to heat, and wet fights with dry, and yet they come together and are not at variance, but they agree, and produce as their result a single body, and the birth of everything.

§37

The same subject continued.

Things then of conflicting and opposite nature would not have reconciled themselves, were there not One higher and Lord over them to unite them, to Whom the elements themselves yield obedience as slaves that obey a master. And instead of each having regard to its own nature and fighting with its neighbour, they recognise the Lord Who has united them, and are at concord one with another, being by nature opposed, but at amity by the will of Him that guides them. 2. For if their mingling into one were not due to a higher authority, how could the heavy mingle and combine with the light, the wet with the dry, the round with the straight, fire with cold, or sea with earth, or the sun with the moon, or the stars with the heaven, and the air with the clouds, the nature of each being dissimilar to that of the other? For there would be great strife among them, the one burning, the other giving cold; the heavy dragging downwards, the light in the contrary direction and upwards; the sun giving light while the air diffused darkness: yes, even the stars would have been at discord with one another, since some have their position above, others beneath, and night would have refused to make way for day, but would have persisted in remaining to fight and strive against it. 3. But if this were so, we should consequently see not an ordered universe, but disorder, not arrangement but anarchy, not a system, but everything out of system, not proportion but disproportion. For in the general strife and conflict either all things would be destroyed, or the prevailing principle alone would appear. And even the latter would shew the disorder of the whole, for left alone, and deprived of the help of the others, it would throw the whole out of gear, just as, if a single hand and foot were left alone, that would not preserve the body in its integrity. 4. For what sort of an universe would it be, if only the sun appeared, or only the moon went her course, or there were only night, or always day? Or what sort of harmony would it be, again, if the heaven existed alone without the stars, or the stars without the heaven? Or what benefit would there be if there were only sea, or if the earth were there alone without waters and without the other parts of creation? Or how could man, or any animal, have appeared upon earth, if the elements were mutually at strife, or if there were one that prevailed, and that one insufficient for the composition of bodies. For nothing in the world could have been composed of heat, or cold, or wet, or dry, alone, but all would have been without arrangement or combination. But not even the one element which appeared to prevail would have been able to subsist without the assistance of the rest: for that is how each subsists now.

§38

The Unity of God shewn by the Harmony of the order of Nature.

Since then, there is everywhere not disorder but order, proportion and not disproportion, not disarray but arrangement, and that in an order perfectly harmonious, we needs must infer and be led to perceive the Master that put together and compacted all things, and produced harmony in them. For though He be not seen with the eyes, yet from the order and harmony of things contrary it is possible to perceive their Ruler, Arranger, and King. 2. For in like manner as if we saw a city, consisting of many and diverse people, great and small, rich and poor, old and young, male and female, in an orderly condition, and its inhabitants, while different from one another, yet at unity among themselves, and not the rich set against the poor, the great against the small, nor the young against the old, but all at peace in the enjoyment of equal rights,--if we saw this, the inference surely follows that the presence of a ruler enforces concord, even if we do not see him; (for disorder is a sign of absence of rule, while order shews the governing authority: for when we see the mutual harmony of the members in the body, that the eye does not strive with the hearing, nor is the hand at variance with the foot, but that each accomplishes its service without variance, we perceive from this that certainly there is a soul in the body that governs these members, though we see it not); so in the order and harmony of the Universe, we needs must perceive God the governor of it all, and that He is one and not many. 3. So then this order of its arrangement, and the concordant harmony of all things, shews that the Word, its Ruler and Governor, is not many, but One. For if there were more than one Ruler of Creation, such an universal order would not be maintained, but all things would fall into confusion because of their plurality, each one biasing the whole to his own will, and striving with the other. For just as we said that polytheism was atheism, so it follows that the rule of more than one is the rule of none. For each one would cancel the rule of the other, and none would appear ruler, but there would be anarchy everywhere. But where no ruler is, there disorder follows of course. 4. And conversely, the single order and concord of the many and diverse shews that the ruler too is one. For just as though one were to hear from a distance a lyre, composed of many diverse strings, and marvel at the concord of its symphony, in that its sound is composed neither of low notes exclusively, nor high nor intermediate only, but all combine their sounds in equal balance,--and would not fail to perceive from this that the lyre was not playing itself, nor even being struck by more persons than one, but that there was one musician, even if he did not see him, who by his skill combined the sound of each string into the tuneful symphony; so, the order of the whole universe being perfectly harmonious, and there being no strife of the higher against the lower or the lower against the higher, and all things making up one order, it is consistent to think that the Ruler and King of all Creation is one and not many, Who by His own light illumines and gives movement to all.

§39
Impossibility of a plurality of Gods.

For we must not think there is more than one ruler and maker of Creation: but it belongs to correct and true religion to believe that its Artificer is one, while Creation herself clearly points to this. For the fact that there is one Universe only and not more is a conclusive proof that its Maker is one. For if there were a plurality of gods, there would necessarily be also more universes than one. For neither were it reasonable for more than one God to make a single universe, nor for the one universe to be made by more than one, because of the absurdities which would result from this. 2. Firstly, if the one universe were made by a plurality of gods, that would mean weakness on the part of those who made it, because many contributed to a single result; which would be a strong proof of the imperfect creative skill of each. For if one were sufficient, the many would not supplement each other's deficiency. But to say that there is any deficiency in God is not only impious, but even beyond all sacrilege. For even among men one would not call a workman perfect if he were unable to finish his work, a single piece, by himself and without the aid of several others. 3. But if, although each one was able to accomplish the whole, yet all worked at it in order to claim a share in the result, we have the laughable conclusion that each worked for reputation, lest he should be suspected of inability. But, once more, it is most grotesque to ascribe vainglory to gods. 4. Again, if each one were sufficient for the creation of the whole, what need of more than one, one being self-sufficient for the universe? Moreover it would be evidently impious and grotesque, to make the thing created one, while the creators were many and different, it being a maxim of science [159] that what is one and complete is higher than things that are diverse. 5. And this you must know, that if the universe had been made by a plurality of gods, its movements would be diverse and inconsistent. For having regard to each one of its makers, its movements would be correspondingly different. But such difference again, as was said before, would involve disarray and general disorder; for not even a ship will sail aright if she be steered by many, unless one pilot hold the tiller [160] , nor will a lyre struck by many produce a tuneful sound, unless there be one artist who strikes it. 6. Creation, then, being one, and the Universe one, and its order one, we must perceive that its King and Artificer also is one. For this is why the Artificer Himself made the whole universe one, lest by the coexistence of more than one a plurality of makers should be supposed; but that as the work is one, its Maker also may be believed to be One. Nor does it follow from the unity of the Maker that the Universe must be one, for God might have made others as well. But because the Universe that has been made is one, it is necessary to believe that its Maker also is one.

[159] Or, perhaps, "innate, self-evident maxim" (logos phusikos).
[160] lit. "the steering-paddles."

§40

The rationality and order of the Universe proves that it is the work of the Reason or Word of God.

Who then might this Maker be? for this is a point most necessary to make plain, lest, from ignorance with regard to him, a man should suppose the wrong maker, and fall once more into the same old godless error, but I think no one is really in doubt about it. For if our argument has proved that the gods of the poets are no gods, and has convicted of error those that deify creation, and in general has shewn that the idolatry of the heathen is godlessness and impiety, it strictly follows from the elimination of these that the true religion is with us, and that the God we worship and preach is the only true One, Who is Lord of Creation and Maker of all existence. 2. Who then is this, save the Father of Christ, most holy and above all created existence [161] , Who like an excellent pilot, by His own Wisdom and His own Word, our Lord and Saviour Christ, steers and preserves and orders all things, and does as seems to Him best? But that is best which has been done, and which we see taking place, since that is what He wills; and this a man can hardly refuse to believe. 3. For if the movement of creation were irrational, and the universe were borne along without plan, a man might fairly disbelieve what we say. But if it subsist in reason and wisdom and skill, and is perfectly ordered throughout, it follows that He that is over it and has ordered it is none other than the [reason or] Word of God. 4. But by Word I mean, not that which is involved and inherent in all things created, which some are wont to call the seminal [162] principle, which is without soul and has no power of reason or thought, but only works by external art, according to the skill of him that applies it,--nor such a word as belongs to rational beings and which consists of syllables, and has the air as its vehicle of expression,--but I mean the living and powerful Word of the good God, the God of the Universe, the very Word which is God [163] , Who while different from things that are made, and from all Creation, is the One own Word of the good Father, Who by His own providence ordered and illumines this Universe. 5. For being the good Word of the Good Father He produced the order of all things, combining one with another things contrary, and reducing them to one harmonious order. He being the Power of God and Wisdom of God causes the heaven to revolve, and has suspended the earth, and made it fast, though resting upon nothing, by His own nod [164] . Illumined by Him, the sun gives light to the world, and the moon has her measured period of shining. By reason of Him the water is suspended in the clouds; the rains shower upon the earth, and the sea is kept within bounds, while the earth bears grasses and is clothed with all manner of plants. 6. And if a man were incredulously to ask, as regards what we are saying, if there be a Word of God at all [165] , such an one would indeed be mad to doubt concerning the Word of God, but yet demonstration is possible from what is seen, because all things subsist by the Word and Wisdom of God, nor would any created thing have had a fixed existence had it not been made by reason, and that reason the Word of God, as we have said.

[161] Cf. above 2. 2 and note, also 35. 1.

[162] spermatikos

[163] Joh. i. 1.

[164] neuma, i.e. act of will, or fiat.

[165] De Incarn. 41. 3.

<h1 style="text-align:center">§41</h1>

The Presence of the Word in nature necessary, not only for its
original Creation, but also for its permanence.

But though He is Word, He is not, as we said, after the likeness of human words, composed of syllables; but He is the unchanging Image of His own Father. For men, composed of parts and made out of nothing, have their discourse composite and divisible. But God possesses true existence and is not composite, wherefore His Word also has true Existence and is not composite, but is the one and only-begotten God [166] , Who proceeds in His goodness from the Father as from a good Fountain, and orders all things and holds them together. 2. But the reason why the Word, the Word of God, has united Himself [167] with created things is truly wonderful, and teaches us that the present order of things is none otherwise than is fitting. For the nature of created things, inasmuch as it is brought into being out of nothing, is of a fleeting sort, and weak and mortal, if composed of itself only. But the God of all is good and exceeding noble by nature,--and therefore is kind. For one that is good can grudge nothing [168] : for which reason he does not grudge even existence, but desires all to exist, as objects for His loving-kindness. 3. Seeing then all created nature, as far as its own laws were concerned, to be fleeting and subject to dissolution, lest it should come to this and lest the Universe should be broken up again into nothingness, for this cause He made all things by His own eternal Word, and gave substantive existence to Creation, and moreover did not leave it to be tossed in a tempest in the course of its own nature, lest it should run the risk of once more dropping out of existence [169] ; but, because He is good He guides and settles the whole Creation by His own Word, Who is Himself also God, that by the governance and providence and ordering action of the Word, Creation may have light, and be enabled to abide alway securely. For it partakes of the Word Who derives true existence from the Father, and is helped by Him so as to exist, lest that should come to it which would have come but for the maintenance of it by the Word,--namely, dissolution,--"for He is the Image of the invisible God, the first-born of all Creation, for through Him and in Him all things consist, things visible and things invisible, and He is the Head of the Church," as the ministers of truth teach in their holy writings [170] .

[166] Joh. i. 18, R.V. Marg.

[167] epibebeken, see for the sense Incarn. 43. 4, &c.

[168] Plato Timæus 29 E, quoted also de Incarn. 3. 3. This explanation of Divine Creation is also adopted by Philo de Migratione Abrah. 32 (and see Drummond's Philo, vol. 2, pp. 56, sqq.).

[169] Plato Politic. (see de Incarn. 43. 7, note).

[170] Col. i. 15-18

§42

This function of the Word described at length.

The holy Word of the Father, then, almighty and all-perfect, uniting with the universe and having everywhere unfolded His own powers, and having illumined all, both things seen and things invisible, holds them together and binds them to Himself, having left nothing void of His own power, but on the contrary quickening and sustaining all things everywhere, each severally and all collectively; while He mingles in one the principles of all sensible existence, heat namely and cold and wet and dry, and causes them not to conflict, but to make up one concordant harmony. 2. By reason of Him and His power, fire does not fight with cold nor wet with dry, but principles mutually opposed, as if friendly and brotherly combine together, and give life to the things we see, and form the principles by which bodies exist. Obeying Him, even God the Word, things on earth have life and things in the heaven have their order. By reason of Him all the sea, and the great ocean, move within their proper bounds, while, as we said above, the dry land grows grasses and is clothed with all manner of diverse plants. And, not to spend time in the enumeration of particulars, where the truth is obvious, there is nothing that is and takes place but has been made and stands by Him and through Him, as also the Divine [171] says, "In the beginning was the Word, and the Word was with God, and the Word was God; all things were made by Him, and without Him was not anything made." 3. For just as though some musician, having tuned a lyre, and by his art adjusted the high notes to the low, and the intermediate notes to the rest, were to produce a single tune as the result, so also the Wisdom of God, handling the Universe as a lyre, and adjusting things in the air to things on the earth, and things in the heaven to things in the air, and combining parts into wholes and moving them all by His beck and will, produces well and fittingly, as the result, the unity of the universe and of its order, Himself remaining unmoved with the Father while He moves all things by His organising action, as seems good for each to His own Father. 4. For what is surprising in His godhead is this, that by one and the same act of will He moves all things simultaneously, and not at intervals, but all collectively, both straight and curved, things above and beneath and intermediate, wet, cold, warm, seen and invisible, and orders them according to their several nature. For simultaneously at His single nod what is straight moves as straight, what is curved also, and what is intermediate, follows its own movement; what is warm receives warmth, what is dry dryness, and all things according to their several nature are quickened and organised by Him, and He produces as the result a marvellous and truly divine harmony.

[171] John i. 1.

§43

Three similes to illustrate the Word's relation to the Universe.

And for so great a matter to be understood by an example, let what we are describing be compared to a great chorus. As then the chorus is composed of different people, children, women again, and old men, and those who are still young, and, when one, namely the conductor, gives the sign, each utters sound according to his nature and power, the man as a man, the child as a child, the old man as an old man, and the young man as a young man, while all make up a single harmony; 2. or as our soul at one time moves our several senses according to the proper function of each, so that when some one object is present all alike are put in motion, and the eye sees, the ear hears, the hand touches, the smell takes in odour, and the palate tastes,--and often the other parts of the body act too, as for instance if the feet walk; 3. or, to make our meaning plain by yet a third example, it is as though a very great city were built, and administered under the presence of the ruler and king who has built it; for when he is present and gives orders, and has his eye upon everything, all obey; some busy themselves with agriculture, others hasten for water to the aqueducts, another goes forth to procure provisions,--one goes to senate, another enters the assembly, the judge goes to the bench, and the magistrate to his court. The workman likewise settles to his craft, the sailor goes down to the sea, the carpenter to his workshop, the physician to his treatment, the architect to his building; and while one is going to the country, another is returning from the country, and while some walk about the town others are going out of the town and returning to it again: but all this is going on and is organised by the presence of the one Ruler, and by his management: 4. in like manner then we must conceive of the whole of Creation, even though the example be inadequate, yet with an enlarged idea. For with the single impulse of a nod as it were of the Word of God, all things simultaneously fall into order, and each discharge their proper functions, and a single order is made up by them all together.

<h1 style="text-align:center">§44</h1>

The similes applied to the whole Universe, seen and unseen.

For by a nod and by the power of the Divine Word of the Father that governs and presides over all, the heaven revolves, the stars move, the sun shines, the moon goes her circuit, and the air receives the sun's light and the æther his heat, and the winds blow: the mountains are reared on high, the sea is rough with waves, and the living things in it grow, the earth abides fixed, and bears fruit, and man is formed and lives and dies again, and all things whatever have their life and movement; fire burns, water cools, fountains spring forth, rivers flow, seasons and hours come round, rains descend, clouds are filled, hail is formed, snow and ice congeal, birds fly, creeping things go along, water-animals swim, the sea is navigated, the earth is sown and grows crops in due season, plants grow, and some are young, some ripening, others in their growth become old and decay, and while some things are vanishing others are being engendered and are coming to light. 2. But all these things, and more, which for their number we cannot mention, the worker of wonders and marvels, the Word of God, giving light and life, moves and orders by His own nod, making the universe one. Nor does He leave out of Himself even the invisible powers; for including these also in the universe inasmuch as he is their maker also, He holds them together and quickens them by His nod and by His providence. And there can be no excuse for disbelieving this. 3. For as by His own providence bodies grow and the rational soul moves, and possesses life and thought, and this requires little proof, for we see what takes place,--so again the same Word of God with one simple nod by His own power moves and holds together both the visible universe and the invisible powers, allotting to each its proper function, so that the divine powers move in a diviner way, while visible things move as they are seen to do. But Himself being over all, both Governor and King and organising power, He does all for the glory and knowledge of His own Father, so that almost by the very works that He brings to pass He teaches us and says, "By the greatness and beauty of the creatures proportionably the maker of them is seen [172]."

[172] Wisd. xiii. 5.

<h1 style="text-align:center">§45</h1>

Conclusion. Doctrine of Scripture on the subject of Part I.

For just as by looking up to the heaven and seeing its order and the light of the stars, it is possible to infer the Word Who ordered these things, so by beholding the Word of God, one needs must behold also God His Father, proceeding from Whom He is rightly called His Father's Interpreter and Messenger. 2. And this one may see from our own experience; for if when a word proceeds from men [173] we infer that the mind is its source, and, by thinking about the word, see with our reason the mind which it reveals, by far greater evidence and incomparably more, seeing the power of the Word, we receive a knowledge also of His good Father, as the Saviour Himself says, "He that hath seen Me hath seen the Father [174] ." But this all inspired Scripture also teaches more plainly and with more authority, so that we in our turn write boldly to you as we do, and you, if you refer to them, will be able to verify what we say. 3. For an argument when confirmed by higher authority is irresistibly proved. From the first then the divine Word firmly taught the Jewish people about the abolition of idols when it said [175] : "Thou shalt not make to thyself a graven image, nor the likeness of anything that is in the heaven above or in the earth beneath." But the cause of their abolition another writer declares [176] , saying: "The idols of the heathen are silver and gold, the works of men's hands: a mouth have they and will not speak, eyes have they and will not see, ears have they and will not hear, noses have they and will not smell, hands have they and will not handle, feet have they and will not walk." Nor has it passed over in silence the doctrine of creation; but, knowing well its beauty, lest any attending solely to this beauty should worship things as if they were gods, instead of God's works, it teaches men firmly beforehand when it says [177] : "And do not when thou lookest up with thine eyes and seest the sun and moon and all the host of heaven, go astray and worship them, which the Lord thy God hath given to all nations under heaven." But He gave them, not to be their gods, but that by their agency the Gentiles should know, as we have said, God the Maker of them all. 4. For the people of the Jews of old had abundant teaching, in that they had the knowledge of God not only from the works of Creation, but also from the divine Scriptures. And in general to draw men away from the error and irrational imagination of idols, He saith [178] : "Thou shalt have none other gods but Me." Not as if there were other gods does He forbid them to have them, but lest any, turning from the true God, should begin to make himself gods of what were not, such as those who in the poets and writers are called gods, though they are none. And the language itself shews that they are no Gods, when it says, "Thou shalt have none other gods," which refers only to the future. But what is referred to the future does not exist at the time of speaking.

[173] Cf. de Sent. Dionys. 23.
[174] Joh. xiv. 9.
[175] Ex. xx. 4.
[176] Ps. cxv. 4-7.
[177] Deut. iv. 19.
[178] Ex. xx. 3.

§46

Doctrine of Scripture on the subject of Part 3.

Has then the divine teaching, which abolished the godless-ness of the heathen or the idols, passed over in silence, and left the race of mankind to go entirely unprovided with the knowledge of God? Not so: rather it anticipates their understanding when it says [179] : "Hear, O Israel, the Lord thy God is one God;" and again, "Thou shalt love the Lord thy God with all thy heart and with all thy strength;" and again, "Thou shalt worship the Lord thy God, and Him only shalt thou serve, and shalt cleave to Him." 2. But that the provi-dence and ordering power of the Word also, over all and toward all, is attested by all inspired Scripture, this passage suffices to confirm our argument, where men who speak of God say [180] : "Thou hast laid the foundation of the earth and it abideth. The day continueth according to Thine ordinance." And again [181] : "Sing to our God upon the harp, that covereth the heaven with clouds, that prepareth rain for the earth, that bringeth forth grass upon the mountains, and green herb for the service of man, and giveth food to the cattle." 3. But by whom does He give it, save by Him through Whom all things were made? For the providence over all things belongs naturally to Him by Whom they were made; and who is this save the Word of God, concerning Whom in another psalm [182] he says: "By the Word of the Lord were the heavens made, and all the host of them by the Breath of His mouth." For He tells us that all things were made in Him and through Him. 4. Wherefore He also persuades us and says [183] , "He spake and they were made, He commanded and they were created;" as the illustrious Moses also at the beginning of his account of Creation confirms what we say by his narrative [184] , saying: and God said, "let us make man in our image and after our likeness:" for also when He was carrying out the creation of the heaven and earth and all things, the Father said to Him [185] , "Let the heaven be made," and "let the waters be gathered together and let the dry land appear," and "let the earth bring forth herb" and "every green thing:" so that one must convict Jews also of not genuinely attending to the Scriptures. 5. For one might ask them to whom was God speaking, to use the imperative mood? If He were commanding and addressing the things He was creating, the utterance would be redundant, for they were not yet in being, but were about to be made; but no one speaks to what does not exist, nor addresses to what is not yet made a command to be made. For if God were giving a command to the things that were to be, He must have said, "Be made, heaven, and be made, earth, and come forth, green herb, and be created, O man." But in fact He did not do so; but He gives the command thus: "Let us make man," and "let the green herb come forth." By which God is proved to be speaking about them to some one at hand: it follows then that some one was with Him to Whom He spoke when He made all things. 6. Who then could it be, save His Word? For to whom could God be said to speak, except His Word? Or who was with Him when He made all created Existence, except His Wisdom, which says [186] : "When He was making the heaven and the earth I was present with Him?" But in the mention of heaven and earth, all created things in heaven and earth are included as well. 7. But being present with Him as His Wisdom and His Word, looking at the Father He fashioned the Universe, and organised it and gave it order; and, as He is the power of the Father, He gave all things strength to be, as the Saviour says [187] : "What things soever I see the Father doing, I also do in like manner." And His holy disciples teach that all things were made "through Him and unto Him;" 8. and, being the good Offspring of Him that is good, and true Son, He is the Father's Power and Wisdom and Word, not being so by participation [188] , nor as if these qualifies were imparted to Him from without, as they are to those who partake of Him and are made wise by Him, and receive power and reason in Him; but He is the very Wisdom, very Word, and very own Power of the Father, very Light, very Truth, very Righteousness, very Virtue, and in truth His express Image, and Brightness, and Resemblance. And to sum all up, He is the wholly perfect Fruit of the Father, and is alone the Son, and unchanging Image of the Father.

[179] Deut. vi. 4, 5, 13.
[180] Ps. cxix. 90.
[181] Ps. cxlvii. 7-9.

[182] Ps. xxxiii. 6.

[183] Ps. cxlviii. 5.

[184] Gen. i. 20.

[185] Gen. i. 6-11.

[186] Prov. viii. 27.

[187] Joh. v. 19; Col. i. 16.

[188] metoche, cf. de Syn. 48, 51, 53. This was held by Arians, but in common with Paul Samos. and many of the Monarchian heretics. The same principle in Orig. on Ps. 135 (Lomm. xiii. 134) ou kata metousian alla kat' ousian theos.

§47

Necessity of a return to the Word if our corrupt nature is to be restored.

Who then, who can declare the Father by number, so as to discover the powers of His Word? For like as He is the Father's Word and Wisdom, so too condescending to created things, He becomes, to impart the knowledge and apprehension of Him that begot Him, His very Brightness and very Life, and the Door, and the Shepherd, and the Way, and King and Governor, and Saviour over all, and Light, and Giver of Life, and Providence over all. Having then such a Son begotten of Himself, good, and Creator, the Father did not hide Him out of the sight of His creatures, but even day by day reveals Him to all by means of the organisation and life of all things, which is His work. 2. But in and through Him He reveals Himself also, as the Saviour says [189] : "I in the Father and the Father in Me:" so that it follows that the Word is in Him that begat Him, and that He that is begotten lives eternally with the Father. But this being so, and nothing being outside Him, but both heaven and earth and all that in them is being dependent on Him, yet men in their folly have set aside the knowledge and service of Him, and honoured things that are not instead of things that are: and instead of the real and true God deified things that were not, "serving the creature rather than the Creator [190] ," thus involving themselves in foolishness and impiety. 3. For it is just as if one were to admire the works more than the workman, and being awestruck at the public works in the city, were to make light of their builder, or as if one were to praise a musical instrument but to despise the man who made and tuned it. Foolish and sadly disabled in eyesight! For how else had they known the building, or ship, or lyre, had not the shipbuilder made it, the architect built it, or the musician fashioned it? 4. As then he that reasons in such a way is mad, and beyond all madness, even so affected in mind, I think, are those who do not recognise God or worship His Word, our Lord Jesus Christ the Saviour of all, through Whom the Father orders, and holds together all things, and exercises providence over the Universe; having faith and piety towards Whom, my Christ-loving friend, be of good cheer and of good hope, because immortality and the kingdom of heaven is the fruit of faith and devotion towards Him, if only the soul be adorned according to His laws. For just as for them who walk after His example, the prize is life everlasting, so for those who walk the opposite way, and not that of virtue, there is great shame, and peril without pardon in the day of judgment, because although they knew the way of truth their acts were contrary to their knowledge.

[189] Joh. xiv. 10.
[190] Rom. i. 25.

www.ingramcontent.com/pod-product-compliance
Lightning Source LLC
Chambersburg PA
CBHW022218050726
47590CB00002B/849